The Accused

The Accused

The story of a professional practitioner accused of child abuse

Richard J. Lewis

authorHOUSE®

AuthorHouse™
1663 Liberty Drive
Bloomington, IN 47403
www.authorhouse.com
Phone: 1-800-839-8640

Published by AuthorHouse   01/01/2013

ISBN: 978-1-4772-3446-4 (sc)
ISBN: 978-1-4772-3091-6 (hc)
ISBN: 978-1-4772-3447-1 (e)

Contents

This book is dedicated to all my friends and colleagues who had supported me through this difficult time, those who have contributed their time and reasoning.

Preface

This book is an autobiographical account of the harrowing events of a child abuse investigation of a professional following a historical allegation by a former pupil of school. The practitioner was a full-time school counsellor who had formerly held the post of being the senior designated teacher responsible for child protection of a secondary school in the North of England. In his private life he had been a foster carer for The Teenage Fostering Team of a large city council. But 20 years prior to the allegation being made, the practitioner suffered a serious spinal injury and had been admitted to a nearby unit for rehabilitation to help recover from a broken back. He needed daily nursing care to help dress, wash, prepare meals, and attend to administrative tasks before leaving home to carry out his work. He suffered serious impairment to his shoulders, arms and legs, and although he can type and drive independently there are many day-to-day practical tasks he cannot carry out without assistance. This story, therefore, presents the psychological trauma for a person who can barely do anything practical for himself, but who nevertheless had to face a series of necessary and statutory procedures following an unfounded allegation.

Anonymous

With the overall interest in protecting all parties, both in terms of the innocent and guilty, the author remains anonymous, and all names of friends, professional colleagues, and official personnel are pseudonyms. All place names and locations, and other identifiable details have been altered to preserve complete anonymity. The conversations and dialogues, however, have been preserved — that is, as far as it is possible for me to recall them. It is the story, and the impact of the story, that forms the substance of the account.

As each day and each episode of this unfolding drama is related, the reader is likely to reflect on a number of challenging issues, and possibly to be enticed to arrive at decisions surrounding safeguarding procedures more generally. It is hoped that this material will not be engaged in passively, but will become an interrogative dialogue with oneself and others from personal experience over such matters, since for this reason the book was written.

The Notes and Arising Issues which stem from this narrative reflect a range of current tensions within professional and legal circles appertaining to safeguarding, but the central topic of the book is the sense of loneliness and alienation with which an accused person can enter when under suspicion of child abuse, and it is this above all else which I wish to convey to the reader. The narrative of what it must feel like to be accused of something whilst knowing oneself to be innocent is a story that is rarely heard in comparison to the many books that have been written on victimology, and it is in light of two recent cases brought to my attention whereby two teachers elected to take their own lives before even a trial had taken place that I have felt compelled to produce this book at this particular time.

Richard J. Lewis 23/09/2012

Chapter 1

A Hard Punch Delivered

It had been an ordinary day and there had been much that had validated my work as a therapist in school. During that day, I had no idea of the storm brewing, or how it would leave me wrecked on a shoreline of isolation.

During the first period I held a counselling session with a young boy who had been regularly teased about his grandfather. I offered him strategies on how to deal with frequent and irritating name-calling. The next session involved engaging with a 13-year-old girl who had frequently struggled with her brother and had a fractious relationship with her mother. Then we had break, in which I chatted with five 14-year-old lads who customarily visited my room for their break, at the close of which I took on two new referrals. An emotive session was held next with a 16-year-old girl who was so frustrated about gossip going around the school and the statement she had allegedly made on Facebook that she was at the point of fighting after school.

In the early afternoon I'd arranged for two peer counsellors to see their pupil clients for a second session. Towards the close of the day, I spoke with a student teacher interested in knowing more about the catchment area of the school and the changing demographic trends of the school's history. She was doing a project at college on adolescent depression and had asked me how many of my referrals suffered from stress and anxiety. I directed her to some of my writing, at which point a penny dropped and in startled surprise she recognised me as the author of a book she had used in college.

On that evening my headteacher Daniel rang me at home to ask whether I would be in so that he could pop round in the hour:

"You're not going out clubbing this evening are you?" he joked. I thought *this seems ominous; he would not usually pay a visit at home. I wonder if there's a staffing issue due to school changes. I wonder if my role may have to change. He obviously needs to discuss a matter confidentially.*

Daniel looked a little apprehensive as he composed himself to deliver the news. He said that earlier in the day he had had two social workers visit him to tell him that I had been accused of sexually assaulting a former pupil. He came straight to the point:

"I've had a visit this afternoon from the area team manager of social services. I had to leave a meeting because he insisted on speaking only to me. He said that a former pupil you had previously supported had been to the police and accused you of sexually assaulting him 16 years ago."

He paused after delivering this punch to see how I would react. I slumped back into the sofa shell struck, stunned into silence.

The most trying period of my life occurred during that summer a few years back after being told that a young man had accused me of assaulting him 16 years ago when he was 13 years of age. During the first two weeks of hearing the allegation I was so distraught I virtually fell apart. My reputation would be now in doubt and I considered taking the easy way out. As I reflect on matters now, I think the only way I coped was through the support of friends and by compiling a personal journal of what I had felt on a daily basis. One headteacher suggested that I should record my feelings to avoid despair.[1]

Chapter 2

Accused of Child Abuse

In mid June, a young man of 29 years walked into a police station, not a mile from where I lived, and claimed that I had assaulted him on a number of occasions in my home and once whilst on holiday.[2] A former pupil and personal 'friend', whom I shall name Alex, had said that I had indecently assaulted him whilst visiting my home when he was a lad. I was devastated on hearing this news—knowing what I would have to go through—yet I was also bewildered as to why he would make such an allegation that he knew I could demonstrate to be false. Equally baffling was the timing of this allegation since he had visited my home not six months before going to the police. This was the second of two visits, in fact, that he had made within the 13-year period of leaving school.

The other bewildering issue was his claim that I had forced him to do something against his wishes. I have a serious spinal condition that renders me pretty well helpless in terms of physically forcing anybody to do anything. Now I know that power is not merely about physical force, but the reader should know, as Alex did, that over twenty years ago I suffered a broken back, and that since that time I have required daily nursing care. I can barely walk unaided or lift a book to my lap let alone dominate an unwilling party.

Alex never lived with me but visited on occasions and would therefore have had ample opportunity to 'blow the whistle' years ago, either to a family member or to another professional, as my story will illustrate.

As a former designated senior teacher for managing child protection cases, I was all too aware of the implications of the allegation and of the ensuing procedures that would take place, procedures that would require me to remain away from where I work and to have no further contact with pupils of the school or any other young person under 16.[3]

The fact is that once an allegation has been made, an unstoppable tanker of procedures is set in motion whereby the defendant will receive virtually no official support, but will experience a most impersonal and unsympathetic series of procedures taken out against him or her as though they are wholly guilty and beyond redemption. The defendant will be left feeling they are a social pariah and will need considerable emotional resources to see the course through. There is also the possibility of media publicity and all the exposure that follows, which makes life so worthless that suicide seems the only reasonable course to take.

Chapter 3

The Impact of the First Punch

Daniel and I had worked together for many years, had a mutual respect for one another and both felt we could be candid and speak openly. It was as difficult for him to make this announcement as it had been for me to hear it.

Still in shock I said:

"Well, that's me finished; that's me done for!" There was a significant pause. "There's no substance in it Dan . . . It's the one thing as a counsellor I can't afford to have levelled against me. I can't see how I can survive an accusation like this once word gets round."

Daniel was fantastically supportive and the next day arranged my legal support. Three senior staff had been briefed whilst the rest were led to believe I was unwell. The local authority had to be informed, and the headteacher liaised frequently with the child protection officials and the investigating officer. Pupils having planned appointments and those who daily supported me were told I was ill and were specifically instructed not to make contact.

Daniel and the social worker had not been entirely procedural in following child protection legislation by the letter — they shared with me the name of the complainant and the nature of the complaint against me. Earlier that day the police had contacted the area social services manager informing him of the charge levelled against me. Almost immediately, he came to my school with an operations manager—I guess just after I had left the premises—and demanded to speak only to the headteacher. Daniel was fetched from a meeting and after hearing of the complaint asked:

"I don't suppose I'm allowed to ask his name and the nature of the accusation, am I?" Suspecting he'd get a negative reply, he was surprised that the social worker revealed quite so much. Daniel, in turn, passed on the same information to me.

It's imperative that details of child protection accusations are not made clear to a defendant before an initial police interview. This is because, whether they are guilty or not, the hands of the investigating officers are tied—the police like to catch a potential abuser unprepared. Knowing details of an accusation beforehand provides a defendant with an opportunity to construct a false alibi, supposing they are guilty. Any pending prosecuting evidence thereby becomes weak. In subsequent strategy meetings, the manager of social services and my headteacher had had their knuckles rapped over this error, yet I guess they both knew this would ease my stress if I knew precisely what it was that I had been accused of and by whom I had been accused (I had known the team manager of the area office for many years, had worked with him on many cases and we were regularly engaged on policy and protocol reform of safeguarding).

What they each didn't know at the time was that through this announcement I was thrown back into complete paralysis again, returning to the ward of a spinal injury unit. This overview had at least given me a narrower focus upon which to retrace my involvement with Alex and to recollect the times I had spent with him, to marshal a counter-attack. For somebody like me the news was not only a shock, it was disheartening. I have given my life for the cause of delinquent and deprived youngsters, the types of kids at school that most find challenging and unrewarding, and to be accused by one such past pupil seemed as much a betrayal of my vocation as a question of my integrity.

My life had become invalidated through what is known in Britain as a Section 47 Enquiry. I knew where such an enquiry would lead, how that in turning over every stone a team of professionals not known to me personally would find cause to be wholly suspicious of my engagement with young people.

I sobbed with the tormenting thoughts of having given my life for hundreds of kids and after having spent a career of 30 years reaching out to needy children, I would now end my days as suspected of being a Schedule 1 Offender, as an abuser of the very youngsters I had served. I would have to undergo the frustration of defending myself to faceless officials becoming my judge and jury, to know that in spite of hearing my account some would still reason 'there's no smoke without fire' — *I thought there was something odd about him. Never to my face, obviously, folk are much too polite for that, but thinking the same nevertheless.*

I sobbed for days as the thought of a new script of my life of coping with spinal injury could be formulated in some people's minds. Instead of the guy who fought the obstacle of paralysis with fortitude and the spirited support of young people, it was only a front to *woo innocents into his lair!*

Living with me at the time was Lester, a 20 year-old lad I had first met at school and whom I had supported through his apprenticeship, and Patrick, a 16 year-old pupil who had been bailed to my address by the court for a Section 18 offence in the neighbourhood. I first broke the news to Patrick. I was aware—even before Daniel had pointed it out—that there was no way he could remain in my home. (Patrick was bailed to my house because he could not live in the area where the confrontation had taken place and because his mother was proud to call on my support through this difficult period rather than on any member of the extended family. On the same day as the incident, Patrick had been to my home with three of his friends to tidy up the garden and to enjoy a barbecue and games of table tennis, but after I had taken him home there was an ugly incident in which he became embroiled with a youth in the area who had claimed Patrick had stabbed him in the back. Nobody believed it, of course, but mine was not the only travesty of justice occurring at the time.)

Before leaving Daniel told me that two social workers would remove Patrick later that evening. This never occurred. This was the second procedural blunder of the senior manager of the case. Patrick remained with me throughout that evening and stayed a further day until 7 o'clock the following evening whereupon a taxi escorted his mother (without any social worker) to my home to take Patrick to his own address in defiance of the bail condition. His mother came into the house to offer me support and to say that she and the family — whom I had known for over 20 years — would stand by me.

On Friday morning the following day, I received a call from Patrick's solicitor outlining his role and plans for Patrick now that an allegation had been made against me. The solicitor reminded me that I had formerly taught him as a pupil of the school. I reiterated the details of the charge levelled against me and he offered me any support I was in need of, whether personal or professional. He said further that this type of complaint was becoming all too common and that it was typical of what they were experiencing as a legal firm: 'it has arisen in light of our compensation culture', that I 'should suspect that the motives would lie in the erroneous belief that he could make money at my expense'.

This gave temporary reassurance until the end of the week when I had picked up further snippets of information, and one detail was that Alex's girlfriend had insisted that he should go to the police to file a complaint against me after an argument between them. This suggested to me that she 'believed' that a gross injustice had taken place in my home 16 years ago and that her boyfriend was indeed an 'injured party'. An alternative hypothesis might be that she was part of the same scam. I started to feel scared since all my experience of managing cases of child protection, which featured teachers in the main being accused by pupils, reinforced a rigid belief held by child protection officers that 'all children making allegations of physical or sexual assault invariably tell the truth', and that despite my accuser approaching 30 and making a 'historical allegation' *he was going to be believed whatever I might say.*

My brother visited over the weekend, but after informing him of the accusation he didn't seem unduly perturbed, not really knowing the implications of such an accusation. My close friends, Frank and Hannah, popped round and gave me comfort and support. By chance, Derek, an ex-pupil, telephoned that evening to enquire after my health. I told him what had just happened.

"Oh shit. I've been there. I know what it's like. There's nothing I can say that'll make you feel better; I've experienced being accused myself. You'll certainly find out who your true friends are," he said. "But ask yourself, what is the worse case scenario?"

"To be found guilty and convicted, and having to receive a sentence of three years in prison." He laughed over the phone for a while. I think I was teasing to detach myself from what was happening, but it was a real fear. He then said:

"You'd find it a doddle. You'd make mincemeat of prison. You'd love it. You'd have them all writing letters to their MPs . . . It would be a new experience."

"Oh thanks Derek!" His attempts at reassurance filled me with greater distress.

Derek was quite a character. He was both academically bright and streetwise, and could keep a foot in both camps. He certainly knew how to play any system and to expose the hypocrisy of some in high office, but he also had a heightened sense of social consciousness. During the mid-1980s he was instrumental in having shopkeepers prosecuted for selling glue-sniffing kits to youngsters in the neighbourhood by assisting me to provide evidence for the police because many of his friends were getting caught up with the habit.

The beating was hurting and each thought and realisation pummelled me with extra blows that sent me reeling to the ropes. Sleep completely evaded me that night—it was a serious punch and I couldn't imagine coming round.

Chapter 4

Mounting Gloom

Over the weekend two social events should have been a distraction but served little to divert my obsessive ruminations. I had arranged a barbecue with some ex-teacher colleagues and shared with some of them the news, and although they tried their best to give comfort I couldn't engage socially in a free and jovial spirit—I couldn't enjoy the occasion. The Sunday should have been the highlight of my year. I had planned to drive my classic car to a show alongside my companion and new mechanic, young Christopher, but this was not to be. Chris had been a current pupil I had been supporting due to his parents neglecting him because of heroin. Not only had Chris been grounded that particular weekend by his uncle, I had been instructed by the team manager allocated to the case that I was to have nothing to do with school pupils until after police enquiries had closed (Patrick having now been removed from my home).

I asked Rachel, my homecare assistant, if she fancied going to the car show and actually help drive the vehicle. I should have been thrilled to achieve my target for the year, a task I knew would be a challenge: I normally drive automatics with power-assisted steering, yet early vehicles had no such refinements. But I couldn't free myself from the burden of worry over an accusation as serious as this one. I must have been boring company for Rachel, but she put up with my monotonous recapitulation of events and tireless deliberations of innocence with remarkable forbearance. We conjectured on every conceivable motive Alex may have had for going to the police, but this had become a futile exercise of fanaticising from all too little information.

Throughout the following Monday my trials of anguish continued unabated:

I am finished. I know I am done. I cannot survive this. I've learned to live for the past number of years with a crap body; now I am to close my days with a broken spirit. The stigma of being regarded as a paedophile was more than I could bear. I felt I needed to build my defence and the first person I could think of contacting was Malcolm. Malcolm was the first lad I had fostered nearly 30 years ago. I had lost all confidence in myself and felt my unblemished reputation was now in question: *how could Alex just walk into that police station and accuse me of assaulting him when my sole interest was to support him?* I rang Malcolm and spoke on the phone and then agreed later that evening to meet up. We drove to a nearby park and sat in the car and chatted whilst children were at play in the distance. Malcolm had had frequent bouts of imprisonment, I believe for 'drunken disorderliness', and I was aware that Alex had received custodial sentences for drugs and car theft, and so felt that knowledge of how 'offenders' view matters would help. Even this rendezvous didn't seem right; I felt as though the eyes of the world were fixed on us — two lone guys sitting in a car engrossed in conversation. I imagined we might appear sinister, as though my attempt to marshal a defence was in itself arousing greater suspicion of the alleged deed I was denying.

Malcolm was consoling and confirmed the fact that I was certainly not a child abuser. He began to speculate on Alex's motive as being centred on money, on compensation. He began to explain to me the 'mind of the criminal', and that people like Alex change from when they were at school:

"You must remember that as time passes in prison he would have become acquainted with how the criminal fraternity work, the contacts made, and that you should not be naïve about his wish to exploit you."

I recounted for him in detail the full story and he, like everyone else, felt that that visit six months prior to making the accusation was very weird indeed and that I should now review it as part of a plan to test my vulnerability, as a ploy to assess my wealth and to plan a means of making money. I replied to him that in my experience his behaviour would not be judged as typical of historically 'abused' young people, and that the police would surely know this:

"Typically, such victims do not feel at ease in close proximity with a person who had violated them in youth, and yet Alex had no reservation in moving right up to me physically whilst reaching for a glass in my wall cabinet not 6 months before. Far from avoiding me and being apprehensive to make contact, he chose to visit me at home and talked confidently in my kitchen."

Many of the discussions I had had with friends and professional acquaintances all centred upon the high probability that this accusation could go nowhere. Everybody kept harking back to 'how on earth could he ever prove in a court of law what he had claimed had taken place 16 years ago', and whilst I followed the same reasoning—which should have given comfort—this was not the central issue of my reflections.

As a therapist, I am interested more in the nature and quality of relationships than in a person's wrongdoings, and whilst I may, according to some of my friends, preserve a somewhat naïve view of human vice I could not imagine how anybody could do this to 'me'. This was *Alex* and *I* had been accused by *him* as an 'abuser'; we had been friends! How could a person visiting an 'old friend', who had supported him 16 years ago, walk up to his house so nonchalantly, with no reservation, enter his kitchen, partake of his hospitality, drink refreshment, engage in social pleasantries about each other's welfares, make promises to keep in touch now being local, and then go out into bright daylight and betray that very same person? That is what hurt most. We had been friends and, although the sands of time had sifted through our fingers, surely everything we had shared together in comradeship couldn't just count as nothing?

My good friend and mentor, Sophie, engaged me in similar reasoning and said,

"Suppose you *had* actually committed an indiscretion in the past with Alex, knowingly or otherwise, it says something about him and his sense of loyalty that he would just walk into a police station when he would arguably have been as guilty of what had taken place as you were, given your high-level disability." She had a point; even though it is accepted that 'power' is not just about 'physical force', I knew what she was saying from a particular point of view. For a moment I had wondered whether she thought I might indeed have been guilty of an indiscretion by framing such an argument.

Nevertheless, I could see where she was coming from. Oh, the fickle nature of relationships.

The next two or three days I *punished myself* day and night, frequently waking in the early hours and barely getting much substantial rest. My greatest fear was where this would lead, who would believe me, and for that reason I kept talking and talking and talking. An old friend from my church days e-mailed me after hearing the news and said that I 'must not fight this battle alone'. In consequence, I spoke with all my friends and spoke repeatedly of my plight. I broadcasted my pain to all who would listen. I rang people and spoke 'openly' about all the details. At one point my morning homecare advised that I should refrain from speaking so publicly because it almost made it sound as though I were guilty — *he doth protest too much!* I said to her that this was the only way I could cope with the mental torture: *I've been accused of defiling a young boy of 13 in my care 16 years ago, and I find it's impossible to live with the thought in my head that some may think I am guilty.*

I kept scanning through my memory searching for hazy details of every incident that could possibly have been misconstrued as an abusive act, every event was scrutinised from photos of us together to see how an accusation could have foundation, but there was nothing! *Could it be that something might have occurred that had caused him to misinterpret my motives towards him? Was there some occasion where I had compromised 'safe caring practice' that had now revisited me 16 years later, something that had taken place between us that had been erased from my mind but which still stood sharply defined in his, a physical engagement that must now be viewed as abusive?* I could recall nothing! I couldn't think of a single occasion where Alex may have supported me in personal care, or helped me wash, carry out nursing, or the like, that he or others now might judge to be sexual grooming? I could not remember a time where Alex was involved in any other way than harmless practical ways like holding my elbow whilst walking or lifting me from a chair or preparing food. Yes there were occasions when he had stayed over night but there were always separate sleeping arrangements. Yes, he may have been familiar with the practical means of coping with my disability (a nature of support that 16 years ago was considered as a commendable, but which today is curiously viewed as inappropriate), but I could think of nothing that could be remotely described as him engaging in personal care, and certainly nothing that could in any way be described as sexual.

The more I re-wound the recording of my life backward and replayed past events where we had been in each other's company the more guilt I seemed to feel, albeit irrationally. Was it possible that I could have abused him and erased the very episode from memory? God forbid. I kept *punishing myself* with this internal interrogation and it was getting me nowhere. I was becoming down and depressed and no longer wanted to live. Again, like before in the spinal injury ward, I contemplated suicide. Malcolm said that I must 'stop beating myself up'.

"You know the facts; you know what took place. The bloke is after money; it's as simple as that." I replied that I was not so sure. His story looked plausible from an objective point of view, not that I'd spoken with the police at that time. I had learned that a dispute with his girlfriend had prompted his visit to the police station. Assuming, of course, that she was not in on a setup, she may be acting responsibly from a moral sense of what is right. If Alex was convinced that I'd assaulted him, then she may have felt compelled to safeguard the wellbeing of all other children that might come under my care by insisting that Alex did the right and proper thing by reporting me as a child abuser. This looked bad from my point of view; it suggested I was a paedophile. *I don't think I can take this much longer – my spirit is broken.*

"Richard", he said, "you are much too naïve. The problem is you see the good in everyone and the world is not like that. If Alex has been in trouble with the police and if he's been taking heroin then that sort would sell their own mother! He will not think as you do. Think of his girlfriend if she has chosen a partner like him to father her child, then what does that say about her? They're just on the make, he's not working and they've no money; it's as simple as that; they're on the make, and you're their opportunity."

My headteacher had received training in judicial matters and one piece of advice he gave was that I should 'take off my counselling cap and think legally'.

"This man is after something and you have to discredit his evidence; you have to fight him and not let him destroy you; don't keep looking for the good in everybody, you'll not always find it." *I suppose they're right and I suppose this has been the most disparaging reflection to date, that my rather naïve and simplistic view of human nature may have to alter to accept the possibility that some will have no limits to make money, even to the point of fabricating an accusation.* As my former student Derek had said to me

"You'll learn who your true friends are." Perhaps too, I should have to reflect on who may become my greatest of enemies in all of this.

I became a little more positive over the next few days, though it didn't last long. I reflected not so much on a past event that may or may not have been misinterpreted, but upon 'what I knew'. What did I know that could be shown as fact? I knew I had never hurt a youngster in my life. I knew I had not assaulted Alex. I knew he could be precocious, particularly when I suggested he should not continue coming to my home. This was because I had felt he was becoming possessive of me and running down his mother and stepfather, being at times jealous of my support of other young people at school. I knew also that although he became upset when I ceased to see him socially, he had become civil towards me in the latter years of school—that indeed he had overcome any perception of rejection and ill-feeling towards me.

I had to learn at this point, as my friends had said, to *stop punishing myself, stop beating myself up* and start—as an ex-headteacher had recommended—having a little more faith in my unblemished reputation, as a person who helps the kind of youngsters few others want to know.

A few days later another headteacher paid a visit and I found her encouragement of great psychological benefit. She began to share with me the fact that over 95 per cent of allegations against teachers go absolutely nowhere, and that in light of the rising escalation of accusations the government was considering a change in law. I said to her that although I found this marginally reassuring, the allegation against me was not a typical one of 'physical assault', where 'hands-on contact' occurs occasionally 'at school', but was a very serious charge of 'sexual assault' by a teacher against a pupil 'in his own home'. This is rare, and in light of current media attention (the school caretaker Ian Huntley had recently been convicted of murdering two young pupils) the investigating authorities were not likely to be dismissive of this charge, nor could they afford to be. They have no course other than to be rigorous in investigating the grounds of the complaint.

"The bottom line," I said, "is that this will boil down to his word against mine." I began to breakdown in her presence and sobbed for a moment. "I've never hurt any boy in my life," I spluttered, "but how can I be sure I'll be believed?" She gave me a hug and said that I must remain strong and she began to share with me the obvious fact that I have to examine carefully the precise details of his allegation and attempt to discredit anything I knew could be proven as false. I began to sob and sob again as I said to her,

"All my life I have dedicated to young people. I've never harmed anybody in my life, and to think that in the end I might end up as a Schedule 1 Offender. I couldn't cope with that; I can't stand the thought." She moved towards me and gave me a further hug and said,

"You must be strong; you have to fight this; you can beat it." She stayed a while and made a drink, giving me time in her busy schedule. Before leaving she enquired whether there was anything else she could do for me. Much to the amusement of colleagues in later conversations, I asked her to put the washing out on the line, and then went to my friends for tea — I was glad to lean on all my friends heavily.

The next day my retired (ex-teacher) friend Bernard paid a visit, fixed my leaking sink, and we had a useful discussion about how vulnerable all of us are in terms of allegations being made in our professional lives when working with young people — particularly youngsters who are difficult and volatile. He lightened my spirit, as he usually did, but then on a different level began to discuss the contradictions and inconsistencies in social attitudes towards child abuse.

"It's funny how if a young male teacher has sex with a female sixth-form student then society would not regard that as offensive as the idea of a male teacher having sex with a male student, and yet as far as the law is concerned gay sex between consenting adults is regarded as an equally valid expression of love as heterosexuality, but people in general do not regard it this way." I don't know whether Bernard's attempts to lighten my spirit through discussions of inconsistent social attitudes helped or not, but it served as a brief distraction.

Another personal friend called by phone the next day to recap where events were leading. I passed on to him the news and shared my uncertainty on how I might prepare for the forthcoming police interview.

"Should I be completely open and honest, and be my normal self, tell them everything about my past engagement with Alex, warts and all? There will be no disagreement over most of what went on, I suspect, between what Alex had said and my version of our friendship. The only difference, I guess, would be over the details of the allegation of indecent assault. He no doubt has made this his central claim and yet I know no assault had taken place." I began to speak freely with him and to talk about my affectionate nature towards kids I had supported over the years. I confessed to him how I would occasionally hug lads and girls quite naturally, or at least lift my arms for them to hug me, and how I might occasionally kiss a youngster on top of their head. But he advised that I should exercise caution in saying too much that's open to a different interpretation—this became a great issue through the proceedings, and remains a crucial one today for carers.

"You have to ask yourself how might innocuous comments be received and interpreted; would it be construed as inappropriate to kiss a youngster who is not your own child?" I wrestled with the prospect of being misunderstood, and thought *there again, I'm thrown into the confusion of how I should speak with the police: to be completely open and honest, as is my manner, or to be guarded and withholding, as everyone seems to advise that I should be, an approach which surely would suggest to the police that I had something to hide. Oh God, why am I plagued with this trial before it has even taken place? How is it that I'm in this ridiculous situation of having to defend myself against a false allegation? Why should I be made to feel guilty when I am guilty of nothing, to be condemned for being who I am—do I have to betray my humanity to be released from this snare?*

Chapter 5

Summoning Support

On the Sunday of the third week, Patrick wanted to make a visit but in view of the team manager's instruction that I should not be in contact with any pupil of the school it's as well that he didn't turn up. A former RE teacher colleague and a past fellow counsellor at school paid me a visit. I related my story and they both remembered Alex, my accuser, quite well (both had taught him in the Special Needs Department). They were not surprised it was a person 'like Alex' who had made the allegation. After I had shown them his picture one of them remarked:

"Oh yea, Alex; he was weird, he was? I can remember him; he was short, wasn't he? You couldn't trust him even when he was at school—he was crafty." Their assessment eased my tension and made me feel a little better. I speculated momentarily that everybody else, and particularly the police would regard him as a suspect witness, the allegation to be bogus, but procedures are procedures, and everyone, irrespective of reputations, has the right to be heard and given justice if a criminal offence has been committed.

Then my reflections became a little more centred and objective, though still pessimistic. *Whatever is supposed to have taken place between us is balanced upon a knife-edge of 'will they believe him or me'. But why did he walk into that police station and make such an allegation? Why would he wish to drive me back into the paralysis of a spinal injury ward? Is it merely compensation?*

Why was he able to pin me down to the ground with the talons of an eagle? Have I hurt him and now it's payback time? Was there an injustice committed years ago of which I am now wholly oblivious? I was beginning to doubt my mind, certainly my memory.

I told them about Alex's two visits since leaving school, and they, like everyone else, said how strange and sinister it was:

"That's odd, really weird."

"Could it be that I have been so completely naïve in assuming he wanted to renew our acquaintance by bridging the years and by promising to call round regularly, as he said he would do, and renew an old friendship? Or was the early visit designed to assess my situation, to re-familiarise himself with my home in order to construct details in support of his allegation . . . to see how he might more effectively destroy me?" *Have I been duped? Was it a crafty manoeuvre? Have I been tricked by the conjurer's hand? Could he really deceive everyone else? Or did he come for some other reason that has now left me baffled?*

"Did he stay long?"

"He certainly didn't stay very long, barely 10 minutes if that, but seemed quite relaxed and at ease." The more they heard the details, the more they became intrigued. I felt increasingly vulnerable.

So I kept wrestling with the issue of motives that might be working in his mind. *How would the police view this visit? Would he deny that it had even taken place? What about trust? That's what hurt most. What about loyalty, about the friendship and support I had given him in the past? Has it all become a means of luring me into a cage? Would not every teacher, youth leader and foster carer, who felt inclined to support youngsters and become engaged with the underprivileged not now feel, in light of my story, that to reach out to such characters is risky? Perhaps we should let things be, let the fate of the disenfranchised follow a predictable course? But then, perhaps, I should keep fighting the fight and not let him win. The cost of passivity is too great. If I am sentenced as a result of being charitable — and at such financial and personal expense — then the knock-on effect has to be a withdrawal of voluntary work, and then who else will carry the marginalised through?*

That evening I didn't sleep, an experience that would be repeated many times. I kept waking from 4 o'clock in the morning till 6.45 when my homecare arrived. I kept wrestling with the prospect of how I would come over during the police interview when my conscience was clear that I shouldn't even have to account for myself at all let alone refute his claim.

Perhaps during the interview I should invite the officer to examine my immobility in every situation — perhaps even in a police cell — and illustrate the difficulty I have in getting around and functioning generally, the restricted movement in my arms and my pathetic attempts at rolling over from the prostrated position on my back. Yes, that'll do the trick; show them practically how I have no power over my own body let alone another person's, but then why, why, why should I have to justify myself and 'perform well' when I know I'm innocent. Remain resolute! Just keep my statement unmistakably clear, deny the accusation and tell the truth.

Over and over again I pleaded to an invisible audience like a novice actor: *I didn't assault this boy! I never abused Alex!* Both he knew and I knew nothing harmful had ever taken place between us. *Why should I have to keep damn well having to explain myself to myself? Who is my judge? Why should I have to prepare for this interview, as though one slip of the tongue, one unguarded comment, might indicate guilt in the minds of suspicious officers and create a false impression of my intentions?*

I had suicidal thoughts again that morning, feeling what's the point of it all? I couldn't really see much reason to continue. My life had little purpose now, no real meaning anymore. My thoughts flooded again towards little Chris, to what he might be thinking, when arriving at school to see my car no longer parked in its normal bay. Wondering whether he would think I had rejected him — like his parents had! *'Why no phone calls? Why no message? Can Richard just be ill, or might he not want to see me? Has he forgotten me and walked out like my mum and dad had?'*

I can't understand all the fuss about voluntary euthanasia. Clearly, it's not about 'taking the easy way out', like some say. I think it takes courage to take your own life. For me, I thought it was a question of practicality. We all see the purpose of life differently according to our circumstances — our economic situation, personal contentment and social wellbeing. We each occupy space and time and have a limited opportunity to experience, be influenced by, and influence, the lives of others, and once that is brought to a natural completion and life has nothing more to offer it seems sensible to end it all, and allow the diminishing world resources to be left for others. *The young people were my arms and legs . . . then again,* I begin to well up and cry. *What's the point of going on if my support is snatched from me.*

A conversation with Clive, a PE teacher colleague, that evening was consoling and this resulted in a better night's sleep, awaking more positively the next morning. I was aware that having young people visit me at home would in itself arouse suspicion for a sceptical mind. I gave an account of why I had permitted young people to come to my home—I somehow felt a need to rehearse anticipated questions that would arise when making my statement, as though I had to 'perform well', as though my fate lay in the hands of my delivery. He replied:

"That sounds fine to me. I think it's going to be alright; that comes over well."

We began to discuss the changes to my routine of enlisting young people to support me in my disability if this nightmare ever came to an end, and although there was no sign I would ever get out of this predicament, at the very least I knew I would not come out of it unscathed. I began to see that things could never be the same again whatever the sequel, with or without my job back in school. The instinctive manner in which I would encourage young people to come to my home might have to be reviewed. Requiring youngsters to assist in walking me around the building for physical exercise may call into question health and safety standards over how pupils might feel should I stumble and fall. Then there was the question of a young person daily helping me for half an hour at the close of the school day. How might it appear to senior staff—merely in light of an allegation having been made—to see me driving off the front car park with a school pupil in a car on a daily basis? I would have to deal with perceptions as much as reality.

Such considerations would be more pertinent now that an allegation had left me marked as a possible abuser of young people; it's not just avoiding any possibility of future allegations being made against me, but it's as much about illustrating conduct that leaves my professional managers, particularly senior colleagues, feeling relaxed about my conduct with individual teenagers in a personal way, especially in regard to counselling clients behind closed doors. *Could I risk everything by being so personally involved again? Should I even put my managers in such a position as to feel compelled to direct how youngsters should and should not support me?*

I began to reflect with Clive my future role within the school as a disabled person. We had discussed many times the prospect of future retirement and how each of us would manage at the close of our careers. I was particularly concerned about the implications of being a severely disabled person living alone whose sole interest was in the upkeep of classical cars. So this kind of diatribe was not entirely novel for us both. Somehow I began to feel no longer the same as I had before. This accusation was going to leave me scarred, perhaps permanently. I said to Clive that I didn't feel overtly angry with Alex; it was more about the system. He was just an opportunist operating from whatever motives were dominant in his mind. It was the child protection system—necessary as it was—that was turning the screw.

As I reflected on what might come about, I said to Clive that I could no longer afford to allow young people to stay at my home, possibly at least until they were 16, and even then not as sole individuals. But then what about the lad who really needed me? *What about young Christopher? He had become instrumental in alleviating my mental torture, but where in practical terms would an accusation leave me regarding young Christopher?*

Chapter 6

Hope through a Needy Youngster

I spoke a little more freely to Clive and other friends about Christopher and shared with them that on the day before being informed of the accusation I had engaged Chris in a very emotive session of therapy. He had sobbed in my presence about the dereliction of duty towards him of his mother through drugs, about his father recently coming out of prison and relinquishing any further responsibility of taking his little boy back home along with his junior brother and senior sister. Hopes were dashed when he had realised that his father went running back to Christopher's mother to cement their relationship through heroin. He lamented how he would have to forbear longer his miserable existence living with an aunt and uncle whom he felt were using him as a pawn to demand a four-bedroom property from the council. Perhaps he was wrong; perhaps he was projecting his hurt on to those who were genuinely concerned about his welfare. I didn't really know.

His experience of them was almost entirely negative, and continually so. He did not feel loved, wanted or even valued by them, but felt they were motivated through a sense of duty with ulterior motives underlying their decision to take all three of them on. How I wanted to take him on and rear him as my son, like so many boys before him, but now, in light of this accusation and what might become of it, I could not even risk contacting him through fear that my motives might be judged as grooming for other purposes than his welfare — what a suspicious world we live in!

But I still wanted to engage with him and offer him a little light at the end of his dark tunnel. We had previously made pledges where he would maintain my classic cars and I would take him to motocross, as I had done with Patrick, when the time was right. I felt he really needed a vision, an incentive, a hope to tolerate his troubles, and I was proud to have given him courage and an aspiration to forbear his current living situation. But now, in light of recent events, was any practical support a realistic possibility? *Should I not be solely concerned with my own survival and put him on hold?* That was Clive's counsel and indeed it was sensible advice.

My reflections on 'life beyond the accusation' had the psychological effect of easing my stress about facing the interview that had been planned for Thursday of the third week, and although I began to wonder what life might look like with Chris going home alone and me being assisted by someone else at the close of the day I also realised that this could only come about through the blessing of his social worker, at the very least.

New thoughts began springing to mind in the early hours as I lay on my bed the next morning waiting for my homecare to arrive. Again a frustrating thought kept springing to mind: *why was Alex doing this? What was his primary motive? Could it be possible that he had really believed I had assaulted him? Was it plausible that he had fantasised over some sexual engagement with me that had become a reality in his mind? Would I have to say to the* police during the interview, *'if this is what Alex believes took place then it must have happened when I was totally unconscious?' That doesn't seem very convincing, but what else can I say if that is what he believed happened?* The thought horrified me even though I knew it would come over as so bizarre and incredible that as a defence it would never be taken seriously.

A military doctor, who knew my spinal injury condition well, had speculated on this in discussion with his wife, an old friend from my youth club days. They rang to give me moral support and to sympathise, and she related to me what her husband had said when discussing the viability of a boy being assaulted by one so paralysed as myself.

"It's inconceivable that Richard could abuse a boy in his care, in whatever circumstances, unless that boy wanted to become sexually induced. Richard has no power or control, particularly when on his back; it would be more probable that that boy would be 'using' Richard for his own sexual gratification; that Alex would indeed be 'abusing Richard'." This I found strangely reassuring in a sordid sort of way, as my thoughts switched between what I knew in reality had never taken place and how a policeman listening to my story might view my defence objectively. *Perhaps he should be my defence counsel if this ever went to court,* I thought.

I found this the most distressing part of my experience. I wavered from fear of whether my story would come over as convincing to speculating on how objective evidence might be weighed. *How can a young person, even one so young as 13, be assaulted by such a paralysed man? It's easy to say this took place; in fact it's so easy to make any kind of accusation if you know that behind closed doors there is only you and the other person together.*

How could his story be authenticated? What collaborative evidence could he provide? How could you prove or refute what took place 16 years ago between two people in a closed room? In a court of law the onus is upon Alex to prove I had assaulted him, not me having to prove it didn't take place. Why am I thinking like this? The fact is I had never abused Alex, whatever he might claim. I knew, and stood grounded in the certainty, that I had never willingly, or unwillingly, hurt or damaged Alex. In comparison, he had destroyed me. My mind also flitted from imagining what Alex may have felt at the time as a boy of 13 to what he as an adult of 29 was thinking now in reconstructing the past.

Thoughts about Chris still came to mind. *What would he be thinking now, having had two and a half weeks of no contact, having been told not to telephone me? Would he have totally forgotten me, having travelled home on the bus, having nowhere to go during break and having no one to turn to at moments of distress, or when getting into trouble at school?* Such thoughts tortured me as my best plans of supporting him had been thwarted.

I had arranged to visit Gordon on Tuesday morning and share with him my current predicament. He was an ex-teacher colleague I had managed in a school-based unit. As I was driving along the motorway, I suddenly thought it would be useful to telephone my cousin's husband, Allen, a retired police detective. He would be a good ally to consult, I thought, one who could tell me how the police first interview would take place, one who could speculate on its outcome from the presented facts. I thought I must return home and ring him as soon as possible and get his advice from one on the inside, most particularly on how I should conduct myself in the interview.

Gordon had experience and knowledge about many things, but I had not known till that day that he had faced a similar charge. He told me how he had felt at the time of awaiting court action over an alleged physical assault. He had been casually walking through a precinct one day and had noticed a man beating a woman. He came to her assistance but her attacker became angry and charged towards him. Gordon put his hand on his shoulder to fend him off, and in effect steered him to the side of his body, at which he crashed into a wall and became concussed. He was drunk. But his partner, instead of expressing gratitude, became aggressive and violent towards Gordon, and had accused him of 'assaulting her partner'. Gordon told me how the pending court case had become a harrowing experience for over six months.

He had elected not to inform his school about the incident; they had no idea what had taken place. So he had the prospect of wondering whether or not he would be suspended from teaching as a result of being charged and found guilty. He related how events moved towards court proceedings, and how at the final stage the chief witness for the prosecution had failed to turn up, as Gordon's barrister had predicted might happen. What resonated with me, from Gordon's experience, was the ongoing feeling of depression. He said that nothing seemed meaningful any longer and how even when friends tried to distract him his mind would keep returning to the prospect that he would have to attend court and possibly be found guilty of assaulting a drunken man.

That is how I felt at the time. Nothing in life was meaningful or rewarding—all joy was gone. I was merely passing time from one day to the next, wondering how I might engage myself, wondering how I could find energy and creativity once again. Little things, such as menial tasks like taking the lawnmower for repair and looking forward to the time when I could drive out and pick it up again seemed disproportionately important and engaging. The challenge of driving my classic car to a show had become of little consequence. I had no one to celebrate the task achieved, the goal won or the enterprise accomplished. There was that lowering, sinking feeling of 'so what!' All was moving relentlessly towards Thursday's interview, like a steam engine shunting into the station.

After the brief call to Allen, he and my cousin, Kerry, paid me a visit that evening—a get together that proved highly beneficial. I related to him the facts and the various communications, together with the lack of urgency to get things moving. He was surprised and said that it would appear that 'they weren't taking it very seriously':

"You must remember that when somebody has made a complaint, whereas years ago you'd use your own initiative and often deal with it straight away at the station, today we have to be seen to be taking it seriously by following the procedures. That's what's going on. If they were taking this seriously you would have been arrested 'at school' and your computers taken away . . . I would be surprised if they interviewed you for more than an hour; it would probably take 20-30 minutes." He explained that when they type up a transcript it is only the salient points that are recorded. The detective would write a report, and the CPS would review the notes and discount the alleged offence as 'no case to answer'.

"You see, nowadays, they're only going to process court action if there's an 80 per cent chance of conviction."

I asked how I should present myself to the police, and he replied that it really didn't matter how I presented myself. He said it did not make the slightest difference whether I dressed formally or casually. I asked whether it would be wise to speak very openly, outline in detail the whole of our engagement and give as much information as I could remember. He cautioned me against this and said my solicitor should brief me on how best to represent myself.

"It's not wise to give information in interview that you're not asked for. If you can answer a question with a simple yes or no, then that's all you should say." I asked whether he thought I should give a context for boys, and sometimes girls, coming over to my home to assist in my disability. He said my solicitor, if he was any good, would advise me on that, but he again cautioned that a lot of information I might want to give would only be relevant if the case went to court. I replied that I could give him a dozen names of young people who had not merely visited but who had lived with me as foster children for periods of two to eight years, that I could give them all their names and contact details and that I was convinced they would support me and confirm that I have never had deviant sexual interest in young boys. He said, again:

"Don't give any information unless you're required to give it; it can prove a disadvantage in the long run. Such witnesses would only be relevant if the CPS decide to take you to court, and although this might not help you at the moment—having to go through what you're going through—I would be very surprised if it went very far. Obviously it depends on what evidence the police have and what the claimant's evidence against you is, but you'll only know that on Thursday."

I asked whether the detective conducting the interview would relate the accusation directly to my solicitor and provide him with the evidence in support of the case against me. He said that that was normally the practice, and that in fact the detective would probably tell me in the opening question what I had been charged with and the evidence in support of what had been claimed, and this would enable me to either refute it all or qualify what had been said. I asked further what type of relationship an interviewing officer might have with a defendant's solicitor. He said,

"That all depends . . . When I was in service I generally had good relations with solicitors, but there are some that you don't get along with, who appear quite obstructive and this can be irritating when you're trying to draw information out of someone who has been arrested. If the officer felt that this was going nowhere, and that they're just following standard procedures, it's likely he'll tell your solicitor that in the first instance."

I found this conversation reassuring and went to bed that night much more at ease than I had done to date. However, I was awakened in the early hours with a nightmare in which I saw standing before me at the police station individuals I had supported in the past. I couldn't remember who they were but there were two or three, and they were equally making claims of having been assaulted by me in the past. I woke up shaking, sweating and feeling highly anxious. *Now, I thought, I am fully exposed to friends and acquaintances as a liar, as one who has conveniently attempted to adjust the truth to suit himself—I'm sure Freud would make something of that.*

I do not know what unconscious thoughts had prompted that nightmare since I have consistently believed there is good in everyone if only we search long and hard enough. In fact I said this to Allen; that my problem is I am perhaps too naïve and trusting in seeing good in everyone, and that you guys in the police force have cause to see more often than I the dark side of human nature. That's my problem with Alex. In order for me to understand his motivations and come to terms with what he has done, I am struggling to understand the question of why? And why now?

Does he have the faintest idea that he has driven me into hell? Can he not see that he has destroyed me? For over twenty years I have had to cope with a pathetic body, and now he's attempting to break my spirit, but why? What did he hope to gain? Could it be as simple as a mistaken belief that compensation was possible from such a treacherous deed? Had he become lured into composing this false allegation for monetary gain? What lay behind that early visit in November that seemed so genuine? It appeared on the face of it that he wanted to renew an old acquaintance, to get together again, to bridge time. There was nothing in my mind that this was part of a staged plan—I don't even think he's bright enough to construct one. So if it was not money and compensation that had caused him to cross the threshold, then someone else must have put him up to it. Yet testing that hypothesis would be virtually impossible. Surely it could not be a grudge after 16 years; that he had felt rejected when I stopped him coming to my home to assist me? Surely it could not possibly be that a person would hold such a grudge for so long, find it still bruising his injured soul?

Sophie thought so and had said frequently that you cannot think the way these people think; we are not of the same sort of people.

There was one further possibility that had encroached upon my mind and this scared me because it led to a possibility that the police might believe his story over mine. *Was it possible that he really did believe that I had sexually assaulted him years ago? Had heroin so scrambled his brain and scarred his memory to such an extent that he was acting out of true conviction? Should he have been subjected to psychological testing?*

Further, if he claimed that I had sexually assaulted him on more than one occasion, then *why did he return?* He was never *made to come* to my home, or to stay overnight; this was what *he wanted.* He was not trapped in a live in situation; *he would return home.* Whilst he might stay for one night in my house and sleep in the spare room he was in his own home most of the time, living with his own family whereby there would have been ample opportunity to disclose any untoward behaviour. I suppose what lay beneath the anxiety of my dream was the possibility that the police would accept his story in place of mine, that he might come over as more convincing than me, that for the lack of corroborative evidence to charge me there might be a chorus of other sufferers at my hand that the police might find who together would decide the issue of counterclaims, and that I was now finished. This was, I think, the anxiety underlying my dream and the distress I had felt as I moved ever closer towards Thursday, the uncertainty of knowing how best to conduct myself during interview.

While speaking with Allen, I had a call from a school secretary colleague asking initially whether I would attend the final school year's leaving prom. In reply I said that it wouldn't be possible. She further asked whether I had been alright for not being in school, in a sort of probing way that left me wondering how many colleagues knew the real reason for my absence or whether she was following an official script. (It's worth saying at this point that my headteacher had elected not to discuss my situation with the staff — a decision which much later on proved to have been very wise.) I was not entirely content with having a 'cover story', but I understood why it was expedient not to publicise my present predicament. I replied to her that I was not ill, but that I couldn't really speak about why I was away. I said that I was in difficulty and that it was not because I was unwell but because of something I couldn't discuss with her at that moment. It looked as though already, as Clive had intimated, suspicion might have been circulating. I invited her to pop round towards the end of the last week of school for coffee and a more open chat.

The telephone rang again shortly after completing this call and it was my classic car restorer. He asked if I could bring my car in the workshop for a re-spray. I replied that I had all the time in the world. These distractions were becoming an escape from excessive rumination. I would never have believed that I could look forward so much to a short drive to pick somebody up, but that's what monotony had reduced me to. *And all the time my children have had to struggle on without me.*

I said to my friend, Frank, the following day that I felt at the time like a man bereaved of his children. He had three grown-up lads. I asked him to imagine how he would feel if a person in authority told him that he should separate himself completely from his children, have no verbal or visual contact with them, and that they would not be given a reason as to why the separation was necessary. And that finally such a separation might last as long as three months, or might indeed continue for all time. That was how I had felt.

What had changed in the previous few days was that I became a little less weepy and more resigned to following a programme towards an unimaginable end. My cousin, Kerry, rang that afternoon to see how I was feeling. She shared with me her reflections on our discussions the previous evening and wondered whether or not Alex had been prompted from a motive of jealousy of my classic cars and perceived wealth, and that he had perhaps visited me to ask if he could loan some money. This was possible, I said, but it had been six months ago he made that visit. She had mistakenly thought it had been more recent than it had been, and then I shared with her a growing suspicion that Alex may have indeed 'believed' that something had taken place between us; that he may have been suffering from a psychotic condition, or been affected by heroin, that had impaired his memory. I told her of one hypothesis I had drawn, which was the possibility that his biological father had sexually abused him, and that he was projecting this on to me, since I was someone he had respected in the past and had become for him, like so many, a father-figure. She discussed with me the characteristics of someone known to us both who similarly might on a bad day be totally convinced of something that could easily be disproved, and that in spite of the evidence to the contrary that person would never back down but be convinced of being right. This, I said, is what I feared most as I prepared myself for the police interview.

I learned that day that Patrick had been spoken to by a social worker, and his mother later told me that she was not happy about this taking place in school without her permission. I expressed surprise that permission had not been first obtained, and that it appeared as though social services were busily conducting their own enquiry alongside that of the police. At first I was relieved that this was taking place — that procedures were kicking in — and that the authorities would be rigorous in checking the facts and that in view of my certainty that there was nothing to investigate then this would help my case, but then I began to get increasingly nervous and agitated.

I visualised teams of social workers attempting to overturn every stone of my life in a vigilant endeavour to discover some ulterior motive for my engagement with lads at home — 'we must nail the bastard!' The social services and teachers generally require a different standard of proof than that of the police to exercise disciplinary measures. Should the police discharge me and close the matter, telling me I had no case to answer, I quite imagined that I would be called in for an extra-ordinary meeting to put before a panel (as a fresh enquiry) my motives for having boys help me at home.

I became angry by the minute as I visualised self-righteous professionals sitting in judgement and declaring that after having examined all the evidence, after scrutinising my life and conduct from every conceivable angle, there was no 'evidence' of impropriety or abuse. *I must be the most examined person in the UK.*

What irked me was that, after conducting thorough interviews with every known young person to have attended my home over a 30-year period, discovering absolutely no 'factual evidence' of impropriety, it would result in a dismissive conclusion. Nothing would be said as I left the room as an exonerated individual.

'And that's it', I would reply, *'that's all you have to say. Having unearthed not a trace of evidence to find me guilty of grooming and abusing countless young people, each of you could not find it within yourselves to recognise the positive contributions I have made and thank me. You would have looked for ulterior motives behind my generous spirit but found none. From your moral positions of ungrounded prejudice you could not conceive that an individual might be genuinely altruistic towards disadvantaged young people and have no ulterior motive, yet you pass judgement on me? How many of you'*, I would love to ask, *'have taken such youngsters into your home? How many of you have supported a child at risk? Which of you have lifted a finger without it serving as a means of career advancement? Could you not find it within yourselves to merely say, "Thank you?" Would it be beneath you to declare publicly that education needs more people like you?*

There is precious little scope if an individual happens to be innocent within the bureaucracy of child protection legislation; the system comes over as uncaring and faceless—where managing professionals are so nervous to avoid personal culpability and to 'cover their backs' when accusations are made that they fail to examine the true motives of some folk without harbouring suspicion and prejudice. This was what angered me most, that these enquiries to search out my motivations of working with young people 'have' to be driven by questionable motives. *Nobody can be that altruistic!* And why is that the case? It's because my life holds up a mirror to 'normal' professional engagement. I do take risks, and I have become stigmatised by those who play everything safe. This is what makes me so angry: it is because my life had become invalidated, like a slow spreading cancer that eats away at a once healthy organ. This was why I first said to Daniel, 'that's me finished.' It was not because I had something to hide but because I knew the authorities would have global disapproval of my lifestyle, even as a disabled person.

All I had pleaded was that they should *ask the kids. Speak to their parents. Let them be my judge and jury, the eloquent determinants of my fate; let them shout from the rooftops my worth. They above all know how to look into a person's heart. They above all know how to judge beyond appearances. They can detect sincerity from falsehood, the genuine from the charlatan.*

Chapter 7

The Police Statement

It was Thursday morning and the sun was shining, but still there was no joy in my heart. The previous night I had the worst night's sleep for two weeks. I lay awake through the early hours apprehensively waiting for daylight to come and felt for the first time with greater certainty that I now wanted to die. I began to think of how I could close my life cleanly without a fuss, and in such a manner that would not disturb those finding me. This would not be easy. *Perhaps I should look on the Internet to see what tablets could be purchased from other countries where voluntary euthanasia was not viewed as much a stigma as it is in the UK.*

I didn't know why I felt at such low ebb; I had lost the optimism of the previous evening in spite of Allen's reassurance that the police would throw the case out. I thought only of the future and of the lack of promise that life would hold. My life had now lost meaning and there was no future. My thoughts were centering on the purpose of my life and of the prospects for all those young people I was no longer permitted to support.

I scanned through my memory bank and thought of Malcolm and how as a single male I had been the first in the local authority to foster a child in care, thereby crossing a frontier, and of the five good years we had spent together. The chips were against him being a success; all I could hope to achieve was to have opened up some potential for him to find happiness and to leave the rest to chance and life's opportunities to do the rest. Malcolm still calls me dad, and has been a great support throughout this ordeal. I knew he was hurting as much as I was.

Then I recalled Graham and how a senior teacher who knew him well had registered how I'd worried about him, and how I had elected to foster him in at great personal cost—I didn't really have the resources or time to support him adequately. He had reminded me that I was doing a degree at the time, but I could not bear to see him slipping out of school and looking so scruffy and ill-kempt, having no support and encouragement to build a future. He achieved much at school, both in his sporting skills (skiing and football) and academically with his examination results. But when Graham moved on at the age of 17 we lost contact and, unlike many of the others, our lives drifted apart. Then there were Sylvester and Ben, and poor old Josh who was knocked over and killed when coming for lunch on Sunday morning. Not only did these lads enrich my life, but I also watched them grow as they learned new skills. They were valued and made to feel important in a world that appeared only to favour privilege. Alex came next—the lad who for reasons known only to him had committed the treacherous deed — and he showed skills in vehicle maintenance, which sadly, unlike the rest, were used for more destructive means than to serve him as a possible career.

I thought of little Steve, the lad I had fostered for four years, and reflected over the many hours I had spent helping him to become more resilient and rise against the pressing gravity of despair from two parents enslaved to alcohol. Steve had a speech impediment. He helped me to remain young, he was funny and engaging, and like so many he gave me a reason to strive against my own disability and press ever onward. Then there were the many more formalised fostering placements, such as Mathew, Merino and John, young people I had supported when fostering had become more regulated and bureaucratic.

Then how could I forget Lester and Patrick, the two lads who at the time had been so caring and supportive? Lester found it difficult to play freely as a child through risks of being bullied in his street; he became a prisoner in his own bedroom. In the area where he lived there was a bully across the road frequently making his life hell, so that he would have to leave early for school or stay safe in his house. Lester moved into my home after leaving school. He learned so many skills that it's difficult to list, and we travelled into Europe three times on holiday. According to his own reckoning, he learned little from school, but I watched him grow both physically and intellectually, and supported him in the essays he had had to complete in training to become, as he is today, a qualified vehicle technician. Lester has flourished with my support, and I did not earn from him a penny.

Then there's Patrick, a teenager whose mother was proud to have had him bailed to my home rather than to members of her family. I had taught Patrick to cope with the stresses of life without becoming angry and violent, and I was proud to see him grow in spite of his recent dilemma.

Was it possible, I thought, *that all this had been to no avail, simply because one man had walked into a police station to make an allegation of abuse?* It seemed so. It was the consequence of whatever action would result from being wrongfully accused that I was finding so destructive. I could not imagine that I would be permitted to accept young people into my home again. *There were going to be permanent scars left from this ordeal, and I wasn't sure I could go on.*

When my homecare came into my bedroom to get me up, she tried to be as cheerful as was her custom, but she could not help but notice my despair. Every attempt to enliven my spirit was thwarted by my negativity. My consistently low countenance had left her unrewarded and every attempt to distract my preoccupation with what lay before me that day was brushed aside. Two letters arrived that morning and the contents of each resulted in switching my mood.

The first was a card from my old youth club friend and her army doctor husband, wishing me well and encouraging me to be strong and courageous. The second was a letter from the teenage fostering team and was a formal correspondence to inform me that in view of the 'seriousness of the allegations made against me' my position as a foster carer was forthwith suspended 'without prejudice'. That was the second letter I had received in the week that had terminated my office of engagement, and within each there was the necessary yet shallow qualification 'without prejudice'. Although I realised that this was what I should have expected, it was another hard punch to take.

What did it mean? Technically it meant what it said, namely that various authorities would not prejudge the outcome of my case, but the consequential effect was to leave me stigmatised, dislocated and terribly alone and unsupported.

The psychological effects were powerfully destructive in that they left me feeling a social pariah.

Patrick had telephoned the previous evening and we had had a long chat on the phone. He was remarkably reassuring for one so young. People were asking him leading questions 'off the record', and it seemed as though from various manoeuvres within the school that the net was starting to be drawn in, the enquiries were beginning to be made, and the investigation over my integrity was underway. I explained to him that this would be the expected course of events, that it would be necessary and that in many ways it was beneficial that protagonists were not sitting down on the job. There was no way my name could be cleared unless officers had completed their enquiries.

This was what probably caused my disturbed sleep. Whilst I would anticipate that course of action as a necessary part of the process, my mind, somewhat irrationally, began to centre upon the motives of such an allegation.

There was a need to 'cover backs', to make sure a paedophile did not slip the net, and to protect all children, clearly, but how much of the driving force stemmed from a bewilderment of the unusual practice of a teacher-cum-counsellor having youngsters supporting him at his home.

Surely, some might think, there must be some ulterior motive? Surely an adult would not give so much time and expense to young people for no personal advantage? Surely there must be something else going on? We must search, and search, and search, until we find that essential ingredient of disguised altruism and goodwill, because it's only when we can find that missing link that we can rest comfortably in our beds within the certainty that nobody in today's world does something for nothing; only then can we feel that our own lives and opinions are justified and the system authenticated.

But what if they were to find nothing — as I knew would be the case *— what then? Well, perhaps we would be left with no alternative but to instruct the disabled counsellor to have no further contact with young people at his own home. Only then, can we consider, as managers, that we have exercised every preventative measure to avoid such risks of further allegations taking place in the future.*

The phone rang and it was Daniel, my headteacher, to wish me good luck in my interview with the police, and his call I found immensely reassuring as I made preparation for the ordeal. My life was on hold; *I was about to have my lifestyle invalidated. It has been a help writing these words, but now my time has come.* I felt like a convicted criminal on death row making his way to the chair. Here we go.

Morris, my supportive neighbour, popped round to put my wheelchair in the boot, and as he did so I had cause to glance at my classic cars in the garage. These had meant so much to me in terms of personal satisfaction and engagement with the youngsters, as my novice mechanics, that it seemed that the battle was about to be lost. This highly productive and enjoyable part of our life would no longer continue. I thanked Morris and drove to meet my friend Bernard who had planned to direct me to the police station. He offered me final words of encouragement before escorting me to the place of interview. On parking the car, I contacted my solicitor by mobile and he came out to meet me and helped push the wheelchair into the station. We soon met the detective in charge of the enquiry. The station sergeant completed on a computer my first police file.

The sergeant said that I was under arrest, and my solicitor in private explained what a police caution meant and that in all likelihood I would be detained in a cell whilst officers searched my property to remove items like my computer for further investigation. I asked how long they would retain my computer. He said that normally it was about two months. I offered him my house keys, but he said that the detective would ask for those in due course. The solicitor held private counsel with DC Henderson, the investigating officer, whilst the allegation was read out to him. Then for half an hour my solicitor related the details of the allegation made by Alex against me. This amounted to sexually abusing him on a number of occasions at home and once whilst on holiday in Scotland.

As the officers DC Henderson and a WPC escorted me by arm to the interview room, they had their first view of my level of disability. All the talk at this point was quite patronising, where I felt talked down to as though one with such a crippled body could never come over as articulate and reasoning. Rather than be offended by this, I turned it to my advantage. My solicitor briefed me on the procedures of police interviews, indicating that he may have cause to intervene should he judge me to be making statements that might jeopardise my case or incriminate me. He also explained that at any point I could speak with him in private session and briefly close the interview. In actual fact, this did not happen.

DC Henderson explained to me that I was being cautioned and he asked me to paraphrase what I understood by the three elements of a police caution:

- the first element is that I have the right not to speak to the police
- the second is that whatever I say may be used in evidence against me, by which I was to understand that any statement recorded in this interview might be used against me in a court of law should this arise, and
- third that I could not rely on in court any new evidence which I chose not to make clear to the police during the formal interview.

I had previously explained to my solicitor—against Allen's counsel—that I first wished to explain my involvement with young people in general, so as not to leave an impression of my engagement with Alex without a broader context, to give as it were an overview of my life in general as a disabled person being supported by young people. I was keen to illustrate the mutual benefits of support; that youngsters, in turn, experienced a raising in self-esteem and developed skills that would serve them in future independent living. I wished to offset a possible presupposition of stereotypical grooming behaviour of a teacher inappropriately engaging with his pupils, or of a counsellor unprofessionally involved with past clients. The complete interview took up three tapes, each lasting 45 minutes, and I felt strangely at ease in this setting. I was surprised to find how easy it was for me to set the agenda for the whole statement, and I felt paradoxically in control. I was allowed to give this overview of my engagement with young people without interruption, explaining that Alex was merely one amongst so many over a period of 24 years who had supported me both in school and at home, and that boys and girls had come to my aid and regular assistance, and that finally such support occurred in five various forms:

- first, there are groups of pupils who bring my wheelchair to the car
- then there are different groups of youngsters who give me walking practice around the school building
- there are some who fetch my lunch
- and then there are others who assist me at the close of each day by taking my wheelchair to a particular location to be charged overnight
- the youngsters who attend my home, of which there had been countless dozens over the past 24 years, have become involved in various activities, which include gardening, home DIY, car maintenance and various visits to places like museums, cinemas, car shows and holidays in Scotland and abroad.

The officers began to question me about my personal involvement with Alex and much of the account that Alex had given to the police I had no cause to question. There were a few details that I quibbled with over accuracy and timing but these were relatively trivial and not material to the accusation. After approximately two hours, and a couple of breaks, the interview finally moved on to the precise nature of the accusation, and whereas I would not confirm with certainty details over the time or events of Alex's general account of our engagement (as related by the officer) which had no particular significance to the accusation, when I was asked directly whether I had sexually assaulted Alex I categorically denied the claim without hesitation. I felt more confident to dispute such a charge and made regular eye contact with the officer when doing so. I felt that he by comparison to me felt somewhat embarrassed to even have to have asked the question. As he related the details of the accusation, one by one, he glanced away at the close of each sentence. Over each allegation, I denied the charge clearly and resolutely.

DC Henderson put to me the claim that Alex had said that I 'kept hugging and kissing him'.

"That depends on what you mean by 'kept hugging and kissing'! If you ask me, 'did I hug him', I would say 'yes', but, more accurately, 'he hugged me whilst standing in my kitchen'. You see, I can barely lift my arms let alone hold a youngster in an embrace." I attempted to raise my limp right arm by way of illustration. "If you ask did I ever kiss him, I would not deny that I may have kissed him on top of his forehead. I have no problem with that." Many of my friends show affection for each other and have done so over the years with youngsters in the youth clubs we had run. We occasionally might hug kids to show affection and demonstrate we care." The officer looked troubled. I had obviously given him the 'wrong answer'.

"Do you not think that is inappropriate with children who are not your own?" In order not to be fenced in, and yet not sell my integrity, I replied,

"I suppose in light of this allegation being made, I will have to review this way of showing affection to the lads and girls I care about," *I wonder if he would have asked me that if I'd have been female.* There was no point in hiding 'facts' with untrue dogmatic pronouncements—like never showing affection—that I knew would not only be dishonest but could be contradicted in subsequent interviews with other young people who had visited my home over the years.

I had occasion to raise the question of Alex's recent visit to my home, and there was a significant pause. I asked the officers if they would like me to continue and speak about these visits, and they invited me to continue. After relating the last incident I was asked by the WPC why I had felt the need to bring up the matter—which I felt was a strange question. In reply I said—with more than a hint of annoyance—that I had found it wholly incongruent that a young man after fifteen and a half years might make what ostensibly appeared to be a genuine social visit, enquiring after my welfare, with an accompanying pledge to visit more often now that he had lived so locally to me, would turn around six months later and walk into a police station not a mile away from where I live and make the most insulting accusation that would virtually ruin me, invalidate my life, and leave me feeling degraded; effectively putting me in hell over the last two weeks.

"How could these two events be reconciled?" I spouted in rage. The officers took note but made no further comment. This was the only occasion I had become animated during the whole interview.

I was asked to reflect on why, in view of my denial, Alex would have made up such a story and have accused me of abusing him. I said that this had perplexed me over the last few weeks and that I had kept asking myself the very same question: *why has Alex done what he has done? And why has he done it now?*

"I don't know the answers to that." Surprisingly, the officers — I'm quite sure against the case of the prosecution — began to give me information that would weaken their case if ever the matter went to court. They explained that Alex had experienced some difficulties in his sexual relations with his partner and after heated arguments he had said to her that he probably could not perform sexually because of something that had happened when he was a boy. He had put down his poor sexual performance to being confused and therefore, by implication, to being psychologically damaged. He was unable to function in a manner that would satisfy her because of an experience he had had with his dad and a teacher 16 years ago. I was further asked what I had felt about that as an explanation — almost as though the officer was not only perplexed over Alex's motives for coming forward, but also as though she was beginning to take my side in the dispute due to the fact that it seemed illogical and inconsistent with a man suffering from historical abuse.

"It makes me feel as though I have become the scapegoat."

"Alex told us that he's still very fond of you, and that he respects you. He still likes you very much." *What the hell is that about? Am I to see Alex as a young man who has sexual feelings for me, to view the possibility that he was once infatuated with me in youth, and, perhaps, review that final visit as him intending not to bribe me but to make a proposition? 'He still likes me very much' — what the hell does that mean?* This confession made me feel even more uncomfortable. There was worse to come. "He said that he was 'aroused' by what had happened. What do you think?"

"I feel quite sick and perplexed in that I must now view that most recent visit through different eyes." *Was I to judge by this that even at such an early age Alex was sexually attracted to me when all I had felt I was offering was friendship to supplement what he had clearly never had with his biological father?*

I said further that Alex had often spoken of an 'imaginary friend' he had had in his early years, someone who had often spoken with him as though he were a real figure, and always on his own during night time.

"Why would he say you abused him?"

"I have no idea. But putting on my psychology cap," I further said, "I wonder now whether Alex was struggling with his own sexuality, whether he may have been abused by his biological father and had elected to 'project' this anger onto me because he saw me as a father-figure who had seen fit to effectively reject him ironically for reasons of practising 'safe caring practice'. Perhaps, during his periods of imprisonment he may have had gay encounters that had confirmed a gay or bisexual identity. I'm speculating, of course; I'm not a psychiatrist." The officer appeared intrigued by the suggestion, but made no additional comment of affirmation or otherwise.

The interview virtually came to a close at this point after I had related to them the nature of my disability, which could be checked by examining the records held in the spinal injury unit during my annual neurological and physical motor examinations. In closing I said that I had wished to be as co-operative as I could be, and that I would give them telephone contacts of significant personnel who could verify aspects of my story. The bail conditions were read out to me, and in closing this interview I was given one further opportunity to speak alone with my solicitor. I asked him how he felt I had come over, saying that I would not hold him to account. In reply he said that the police would obviously check isolated details of what I had said and that should they not find any significant disagreement or contradictions I should be OK.

"You came over as being open and honest. The CPS will read the case notes and will examine the weight of evidence they think exists to secure a conviction, and whether or not it would be 'in the public interest' to charge you. My guess," he said, "is that they will throw the case out."

"Do you think it would serve my interest if I resigned my post at school so that the 'public interest' could be served with me no longer having regular contact with young people?"

"Certainly not!" he replied. "You should do nothing; this would not help your case." My bail date to return to the station was set for the end of August, and I was informed that should the particular CPS lawyer, who was likely to look into my case, judge it to be 'no case to answer' then I would hear by telephone before that set date, with a letter of confirmation to follow.

I felt remarkably relaxed after the interview, and on reflecting on the officers and my solicitor managing and supporting me in the interview I thought they looked more tired than I did by comparison—I felt quite energised and relieved after the ordeal. As I mused on the experience, it surprised me how much I had felt in control of the entire situation. I felt I had got across my character and lifestyle in the way I wished my involvement with youngsters to be seen and that my anxiety at this point should now diminish. I could switch off my tap of worry, since there was nothing I could do to settle my fate either way.

I engaged in an objective mental exercise during my drive home, of stepping outside myself in order to perceive the case for and against my innocence. I looked at the evidence from the police point of view. First, I considered the plausibility of my own testimony and naturally it appeared OK to me; from an-all-too subjective stance, I came over as quite plausible. I had accounted for why I had stopped him coming and speculated for the police, at their request, a motive for his accusation. I felt I was purposely vague in areas where I felt uncertain, and that I was convincing in those where I could recall clearly the facts.

I then attempted to objectify my experience and to look at the two narratives from the perspectives of the police officers. How would they view Alex's story? Well, it seemed plausible in one sense, and we have to reckon with the fact that he had come forward, in spite of a voiced 'liking' and 'respect' for a person he was accusing, and in light of the fact that as an ex-offender himself he would have an instinctive reticence to cooperate with the police, albeit sexual offences against children are viewed even by the criminal fraternity as objectionable, perhaps even more so by them. Here was a young man who had experienced sexual dysfunction and through arguments with his current partner, and mother of his child, had felt a need to account for his problems, and how better than to put it all down to first his father then to a teacher who had abused him 16 years ago in youth. From such a position, his girlfriend would push Alex to do the noble deed so that at the very least the authorities could safeguard the possibility of others being abused by this man in his home — all very plausible, and with no monetary incentive.

What about my story? Here is a teacher and youth counsellor who had taken an active interest in young people over many years and had become attached to Alex, a lad in need of an ideal father-figure. Being disabled, mutual support was had in an open manner with each of their respective families and friends, who were cognisant of the engagement. As this relationship outgrew and presented more difficulties than benefits, with a too-clingy element arising in such an attachment — at least from one party's point of view — the accused attempted to extricate himself in order to exercise 'safe caring practice'. In doing so, the youngster took exception, became angry, bore a grudge and nursed bitterness for a short while. This appeared to have been resolved in time, which left a riddle as to the true purpose of his visit six months before the accusation was made. Being an unreliable witness, having served time in prison for car theft and heroin misuse — a life-story that compares not well with the unblemished record of the accused — we have to account for motives and what Alex might gain from a possible trial and conviction. *Might it be a possible compensation claim, or a plan to bribe the defendant to withdraw his allegation and stop the case going to court? Might it be confused thinking from an addict with no sense of loyalty or commitment to anybody or anything but his next fix? Or might it just be a need to account to his girlfriend for his current sexual dysfunction in spite of him at least being once able to get her pregnant?* Again, this alternative version can appear plausible (if hypothetical) without more known facts surrounding his situation. In essence, *was I being used as a scapegoat or a possible means of future compensation?*

On arriving home, I was glad to see my homecare waiting in her car for me to arrive. She assisted me in preparing my tea, but then later returned to finish the job and to enquire on how I had got on at the police station. I arrived home by about 8.00 p.m. and the telephone rang perpetually, but I did not feel like taking calls that evening and retired early to bed. I did, however, give Daniel a call to report back and he said that it seemed as though I'd had a satisfactory interview. I said that I had felt a little more relieved now that it had taken place. I began to reflect on why the interview appeared to have gone so well in light of my previous apprehension. I think it was due to my preparation and to the fact that I had taken on board elements of advice given by various people.

Although Allen had suggested that I should say very little to the police and not qualify answers if a yes or no would do, that the least I said the little they would have to scurry around in seeking evidence that would confirm or contradict my statement, Daniel, my headteacher, had suggested that I should be open and honest during the interview. Another friend had similarly advised that there may be features of my honesty that could be misconstrued during a formal interview with officers who did not know me as my friends had known me. All in all, I think I took a middle course in balancing the various pieces of advice I had been given.

My solicitor did not override my wish to give an overview of the context of working with young people—the context of my involvement with lads from school coming to my home. Various friends had advised differently on the appropriateness of becoming angry, or emotive, during the interview. But my decision was to remain calm and reasoned throughout with no changing intonation or pausing when reaching critical parts of the allegation.

I actually rehearsed the type of questions I had anticipated would be asked during the interview. I didn't want officers misreading, or reading into, anything I had said. I was nervous enough about the whole enterprise anyway, and suspected that parts of the intimate sexual details I would find abhorrent and offensive and that I might give a false impression through anger that might imply guilt or covering something up.

This preparation helped me remain calm and contained, and in consequence to come over more confidently. It might be reasoned that such preparation should not be necessary, that honesty and innocence comes through in the end; that truth always prevails. This may be so, but we're only human, and facing searching police officers' eyes across a desk with recording equipment designed to capture every word, nuance and expression over hazy details of as long ago as 16 years, that effectively determines one's liberty, is not entirely the most comfortable of situations in which to be.

Chapter 8

'Safe Physical Touch'

Morris popped round early the next morning to find out how I had got on at the police station. We were experiencing wet weather at the time and there had been various local floods up and down the country, especially in Yorkshire. I had planned to visit Sophie, an ex-teacher colleague, that day and Morris advised that I should look on a map and telephone her to enquire whether reaches of the local river were passable. She reported that the river had gone down where I would cross, and that my journey would be fine. I set out on a sunny day as it happened and felt that the world looked a bit brighter.

Travelling through the various villages towards her house was always pleasant and scenic, and she had always been a comforting soul mate with whom I could confide. She listened attentively to my account of the interview and responded to the various statements of the officers as filtered through my recollections. She seized upon that part of the police reply that gave the key to the missing riddle. Sophie had more insight into adult sexual relations than me, particularly over the wiles of flirtation.

"There's your answer," she said. "It's always the same with men like him. Things that go wrong in life are never their fault. There's got to be someone else to blame. He's having sexual problems with his girlfriend, and it's all your fault!"

I must admit that I had not seen the picture as clearly as she had done, but there was part of me wondering whether Alex had gay inclinations and had had fantasies of a retrospective past engagement with me; that, perhaps, he may have been struggling to come to terms with the fact that he may be gay or bisexual.[4] I further said to her that I had wondered whether he may have had same-sex encounters, willingly or enforced, whilst in prison.

There was one other reflection on the interview that resulted in a humorous response from her. I recounted that part where the detective seemed concerned about my tendency to hug a lad or a girl known well to me from school, and even kiss them occasionally on the forehead.

I freely volunteered this information after I was asked whether I had kept hugging and kissing Alex by the interviewing officer. Now, I have no ethical problem with showing affection to young people in such a manner.[5] 'Safe touch' I think is important in helping youngsters — particularly those who are deprived of affection—to reduce a sense of alienation and isolation. Clearly, the detective did not agree and said so in reply:

"Do you not think that is inappropriate with children who are not your own?" My personal conviction was and still is: 'No, I damn well don't think it's necessarily inappropriate.' I would love to have said: *'Would you have asked me that question if I were a woman?'* I further said to her that the detective visibly raised his eyebrows at my confession, as though I had given 'the wrong answer', but conventions 16 years ago—from which I should, but probably would not, be judged — were not as restrictive as current child caring practice. DC Henderson and his WPC colleague were much younger than me. Sophie grinned in agreement, recognising their pomposity and gender stereotyping, and said,

"Well, why am I not surprised at that? The police are not exactly renowned for getting in touch with their feminine side are they?" We both laughed, and when I related this comment to another headteacher known to us both, she also laughed and said, 'I can imagine Sophie saying that.'

Showing physical affection was the one feature of my statement that left the officers uneasy, and remains an issue for professionals and foster careers to this day. As I review this script now, I recognise how I will appear naïve and how such a demonstration of affection will be viewed after being accused of abuse and in light of current attitudes over circumspect behaviour between teachers and pupils, but 16 years ago conventions and attitudes were more relaxed and arguably less hung up than they are today.

In spite of the obvious recognition that paedophiles might groom children by such subtle manoeuvring, genuine caring is visibly displayed in such a manner, and here is the problem! Young people, unmistakably, are able to give feedback through word or gesture if they feel that hugging them is unwanted or outgrown, and the 'responsible' adult should respond accordingly. I would not lie to the officer, even though I knew it would jeopardise my position, not only because in principle I would not be happy with myself through so doing, but also because I would be found to be withholding information that would come out in subsequent interviews with lads should this occur.[6]

The drive home was pleasant although I was running late for tea at my good friend's Jason and Mary. As I pulled off the drive, the sight of a cock and hen pheasant striding purposefully along the country lane with their three offspring moved me with compassion and loss. The little family looked so humorous, so colourful and innocent, so lovely and together, so at one, and it lifted my spirit to possibilities of renewal. They appeared not to have a care in the world; how much I envied them.

The issue of physical contact with children and young people has perhaps raised the most debate amongst friends in follow-up discussions over my case, and it is an issue in which foster carers are constantly wrestling. I shared the information with my classic car renovator and with Jason and Mary (all of whom were foster carers) during a meal one evening. My renovator said that we constantly bring this up with our support workers and they give ambivalent messages, normally advice that is impractical to adhere to. Jason and Mary had recently been trained in 'safe-caring practice' as foster parents and they told me the current guidance on the issue. In regard to 'safe-physical touch', they were advised not to allow children to hug them in a frontal position.

"We are instructed to move the child to the side of our bodies if we are standing, and to hold them close to the waist and give them a hug, obviously, away from the genital area." Jason demonstrated — it was like steering the child as a matador would a bull. I observed Jason and Mary both hugging and kissing their foster children (one 11 and the other 9) goodnight whilst sitting on the sofa, naturally though in defiance of recommended practice. They acknowledged how impractical the guidance was. It seems as though key workers in foster care are reluctant to give assent to hugging and kissing children and young people in arguably natural ways through fear of giving licence to something that may leave them culpable as managers in potential cases of historical allegations. I suppose it is to avoid a possibility of giving legitimacy to a practice or routine of a carer towards a child in the event that that child may make an accusation of abuse against his or her past carer. In other words they do not want to leave themselves open during enquiries of an offence in which a carer can claim in their defence that their key workers had approved of holding, hugging or kissing a child without qualification.

But I would say it is imperative that we make measured affectionate contact with children and young people within safe boundaries; that it is impossible for them to learn how to be affectionate and caring towards others if they have not received the same during their childhoods.

I arrived home late that evening and found 10 telephone messages on my answer phone. I decided to stay in the next morning and respond to the various friends who were anxious to know how I had got on during the police interview. After making the various calls, I got ready to join friends in celebration of Frank's 60th birthday barbecue later that evening. I had elected not to speak at length about my situation since this would not be the appropriate time or place but would plan to visit various groups of friends over the next few weeks and share with them how I had got on.

Towards the end of the evening, I spoke with Frank's mum and dad, now in their eighties. They recalled memories of Frank and me in youth at their home and reiterated anecdotes of times I had played the guitar for groups of singing young people. For a fleeting moment, I recalled the times of my early twenties and pondered again that vexing question of *should all my life be rendered insignificant in light of the possibility of ending up a Schedule 1 Offender?*

The following day was largely uneventful, apart from a few calls to friends and a further visit from Kerry and Allen, the retired police officer. I shared the details of the police interview and the subsequent bail conditions and invited his comment. He replied the same as before, that I should feel more assured; that in his judgement the police would not take the accusation seriously, that all the signs were against it being high priority:

"If I were dealing with your case the enquiry would be closed long before the end of August." Again, I found this incredibly reassuring as I weighed up the facts as they stood out in my mind. If Allen would prove correct by saying that the CPS lawyers required 80 per cent likelihood of a conviction, then the odds were in my favour. If the central issue would be my word against Alex's, then that results in a 50-50 per cent equation. Then add to that the nature of my disability and the feasibility of being able to perform what he had claimed I had done, then that tipped the scale lower on Alex's side. Add to that my unblemished career of working with so many youngsters in comparison with his past addiction to heroin and criminal offending then the balance lowered further. Then add to that a hypothesis of an excuse for sexually poor performance, or perhaps monetary gain, as a motive for Alex to have made the complaint then I should free myself of all worry. *So, why was I still so incredibly anxious over a possible prosecution?*

I suspect it had something to do with the fact that it was inevitable for my friends to tell me what I had wanted to hear. After all they know me well. But I would be judged — and my fate would be held in balance — by others who would not know me and whose role and experience would cause them to be suspicious of adults in my position behaving so sociably with pupils from school. After all, my cousin's husband, friends and fellow professionals didn't *really* know what had happened between Alex and me; they could only trust my word and view me according to the altruism they had observed over the years; it was only we who knew what *really* had or had not taken place in the privacy of my home 16 years ago.

Added to which, my feelings were 'my feelings', not anyone else's, and I suspected — or had at least imagined — that Alex had not for one moment batted an eyelid, or even given a single thought, to the effects of his deed, a deed which by contrast had driven me to despair.

His motive may centre on opportunism or saving face with his girlfriend — who will ever know? I fantasised that he carried no sense of guilt over what he'd put me through — how could he in a system where advocacy swings unreservedly towards a 'plaintiff' of abuse and where claims of abuse are normally accepted without question. I know I am free of guilt, and it concerns me that Alex knows his charge is bogus.

So why am I filled with doubt and uncertainty? I suppose it all centred on the fact that I was not confident in the current child protection procedures in light of what I had experienced in managing the cases of others who had been in the same position I had now found myself. *If this was going to be thrown out in the final analysis, then why oh why do I have to suffer the torment of waiting for a decision that is likely to take at least three months?* Surely, it could have been closed in a matter of three or four weeks, not three or four months. Allen said in reply that when he was at the station he tended to do the same.

"We want to give ourselves plenty of time so that we can close a case with all the extra demands that come our way. We can't fully predict what offences will happen on a daily basis. We have to give ourselves plenty of time to carry out the initial investigation, do all the interviewing, get all the paperwork in to the CPS."

"But that's not fair!" I said in reply. "It puts the accused through unnecessary torment."

A discussion of potential allegations being made against professionals was taken up with one of my morning homecare workers when she began to express her anxieties over her son (currently teaching in a special school). She saw it as a real possibility because he was young, tall and a good-looking chap. She had read somewhere that they were struggling to get male teachers to work in primary education and pondered whether fear of allegation was driving many would-be young male teachers away as a result. I further talked of a friend of mine aged 70 who when out walking his dog would now turn away from playing young children, when years ago he would smile at them, perhaps talk and even engage with them in jovial horseplay. This was just in case his forwardness was misinterpreted as grooming.

"It just seems to me," I further said, "that our age has become schizophrenic in regard to sexuality. We have explicit sex thrown at us through television, film and the Internet. Then we have puritanical attitudes towards the slightest gesture of affection shown to children by caring people. And then we have a systematic withdrawal of support when an accusation is made, whether founded or unfounded, by professionals keen to 'cover their backs' and preserve their own culpability through distancing. Children need 'loving touch' and affection, and carers and teachers have become paralysed with fear over how they can express care and concern without being subjected to misinterpretation and possible later allegations of abuse. What a crazy world we live in."

Chapter 9

The Monotony of Waiting

I telephoned Patrick late on Sunday evening and gave him a much fuller account of my interview at the police station. I shared with him my worries about Chris, and speculated that in view of my situation the door might have to close in directly supporting him from now on. Obviously, he could not comment, but pledged himself to offer any support he could with arrangements after school 'when I came back'. He also said that if he had the opportunity he would like to move in again when it was all over. I said we should have to consider that later on, and I further said that my neighbour was still keen to call on him and pay for his labour in the first few weeks of the school holidays if he were still willing (he wanted to be a builder after leaving school and my neighbour was building a garage extension). He replied that he was.

I had to telephone my headteacher again to give further information he needed to close the enquiry quickly and to plan some damage limitation with the after-effects in terms of my work in school when multi-strategy conferences had closed—everyone consulted was still expecting the case would be thrown out and myself reinstated in the very near future.

My two friends, Melanie and Jack, had invited me for dinner the following Monday and the drive out was a fitting break for the day. I shared with them the main elements of my ongoing story but by now I was getting tired of going over the same material with each new audience. Fresh insights into my dilemma and renewed conjecture on Alex's motivations were becoming less frequent and I was becoming bored with it all. I suppose it may have been something to do with a need to keep justifying myself, yet I later felt this was becoming pointless and unnecessary. The simple facts still remained, in my judgement: I had been accused of sexually assaulting a 13 year old boy 16 years ago and yet he and I knew this had not taken place. Some may believe me; others will hold me in suspicion. I resolved a pragmatic course, since I reasoned that I have no control over what people think!

The way the case was moving seemed to suggest to all my friends that there would be no charges made or any prosecution for me to face. I took this up with Melanie and Jack and said there were two layers of concern that weighed upon me heavily. In one sense having to go to court wasn't a worry. I suspected, although I could not be too presumptuous, that this would not go to court, but should this be the sequel and I were judged innocent — even though it may have given relief — the cloud that hung over my head would still not have been removed. I explained to Melanie that the damage for me was that *Alex had accused me of obscene acts*, which, not only offended my sensibilities, it had left me feeling vulnerable about any further contact with young people.

What I wanted was something I knew would never take place. I wanted Alex to go into the very same police station and withdraw his statement and explain that there was never any substance in what he had said. But this would have been highly unlikely to take place — how could he retract?

The die had been cast: he would lose face, look foolish to his supporters, and possibly be charged for wasting police time.

I was left with a dilemma of knowing that those having a legal responsibility would suspect that I might still be responsible for doing something obscene, but that it simply 'could not be proved', not 'beyond all reasonable doubt'. So, although I might avoid prosecution, I would not necessarily escape suspicion. I think this was the reason why when driving home sadness invaded my spirit to such an extent that a part of me felt, *Sod it; take me to court if you will. Find me guilty and send me to prison if that's what you want!*

On entering the house I noticed that a message was left on the answer-phone and it was from Malcolm. I wondered whether the police had contacted him for a statement, since, with his agreement, I had given them his number. After making a cup of tea, I gave him a call; it was insignificant, he wanted to use my classic car for a relative's wedding. We discussed again my dilemma and he shared with me his later deductions, which seemed to move in the same direction as my growing assumptions.

I said to Malcolm that I was wondering whether Alex was bisexual, and that he may be struggling with his sexual identity. Malcolm confirmed that this was becoming his and his partner's conclusion, that Alex had experienced difficulty in sex relations with his girlfriend, not finding sex satisfying owing to a denial of his gay orientation. I shared with him extra detail that the police had surprisingly disclosed to me, which was that Alex had said to them that he was 'fond of me', that he 'still likes me ', that he 'respected me' and that he claimed to have been 'aroused' in my company. Was he telling the police that I had 'made' him gay, and that this was the reason why he could not have fulfilled relations with his girlfriend? Surely not!

I said to Malcolm that this would only make sense if indeed there had been a sexual relationship between us, but no such thing had ever taken place. Is it possible that Alex at the age of 13 may have fantasised over an imaginary sexual relationship between us? Malcolm felt this was feasible, yet, although I knew Alex had had an active imagination (his 'imaginary friend' etc.), I couldn't see him needing to invent such a story without a clear motive. Malcolm concluded that whatever had been the answer 'you can bet your life that money lies at the root of it'.

"Somebody has put him up to this and I wouldn't be surprised if his girlfriend is involved; it's about compensation." Given that Malcolm had spent frequent periods of his life in prison, and in police stations having to answer pressing questions in interview, I was keen to ask him one further question.

"From your experience, Malcolm, if a young man had served time in prison for car theft and heroin misuse, say, having to dodge authority many times over to avoid prosecution, how easy would it be for such a person to walk into a police station and accuse a past acquaintance of an offence against him?"

"Virtually impossible," he replied. "You want to keep well away from the police; you don't want to grass on others, whatever they'd done when you've been in trouble with the law." (Mary in a later discussion said, "They couldn't be certain they'd be believed.")

"That's my problem. But what about sex offences against children?"

"Oh, that might be different . . . but then he knows you!"

"But there's my dilemma. He's going to be believed, isn't he? At least, taken seriously", I said. "Alex has crossed a threshold and gone into a police station to accuse me of a shameful act against his person, and to somebody he has claimed, and, paradoxically, still claims, to be 'fond of', someone 'he still likes' and 'respects'. I am left bewildered, not just dispirited. He's either playing a game for an unknown reason, mentally deluded, or driven by a dominant partner with no scruples. Whatever the case, he's completely oblivious to how his accusation is destroying my life?"

I said to Malcolm that his message on the answer-phone had left me wondering whether the police had made contact. His reply was not as yet, but that I did not have to worry:

"I'll tell them the sort of person you are. Living with you was the happiest time of my life, and I will never forget that. You don't deserve what you're going through, but you have to realise that 'the police are just doing their job and it takes time'." I told Malcolm that he may have to expect some intrusive questions, and I related to him what the social workers had enquired of Patrick. I was expecting them to ask him about sleeping arrangements in place at our home whilst he was there. In fact, this did not occur. Malcolm replied that I should not worry, that when the time came he would tell the truth.

When Patrick had been questioned, or, more accurately, 'interrogated', by a social worker, he had been asked what he would do if an adult had touched him between his legs down below. His reply was that he would tell his mother.

"Who else would you tell?" the social worker further enquired.

"I would tell Richard." Somewhat startled (noticed Patrick), she asked:

"And why would you tell Richard?"

"Because I trust him." When Patrick related this it brought me to tears. I felt validated. He could not have given them a better testament to my character, yet his response left them thrown off course. Perhaps, my ex-headteacher had been correct after all when he had said that I should 'start believing in myself'.

Why then did I feel so doubtful, with so many friends coming to my support, whom in the final analysis were only 'telling the truth?' I think it was because deep down *I did not trust the system*. I was made to feel guilty and ostracised. I was aware of all the sceptical discussions going on behind my back, simply because of the snippets of information that were filtering through. Daniel rang me that morning to say that the police had sent him a fax asking him to send them a copy of my job description and the protocols of operation when youngsters 'are placed with me'. Daniel's reply was that, apart from the job description, he didn't fully understand what was being asked of him, because it seemed to be a request about 'fostering children' not about 'clients engaged in school counselling'.

Although I had recognised that it was absolutely necessary that these enquiries had to take place, and take place quickly for my benefit, it still didn't stop me feeling uncomfortable, knowing that professionals were searching for evidence of malpractice, and leaving not one stone unturned, in trying to find information that might suggest that I had a covert sexual interest in boys in my care. It was disconcerting to know that officers were searching files and asking all sorts of leading questions of young people I had previously fostered. In frustration, I'd inwardly groan: *when will the accused become free?*

I reflected on the questions asked of Patrick over a cup of tea, and then it hit me what was really going on. What they had been trying to elicit from Patrick was whether he would 'tell anyone' if I had been abusing him in my home. His reply that he would tell his mother was natural enough, but to add that he would also 'tell me' would throw the interrogators into confusion. By declaring that he would also 'tell Richard' — because 'I trust him' — would have had the effect of closing all further questioning. They would not have anticipated that. *Time to search elsewhere for 'evidence' that I might be a 'grooming pervert' – 'abuser of young boys'. Somehow I got the feeling that the enquiring authorities could not come to terms with the 'fact' that I might want to help lads for no ulterior sexual motive.*

The following day Frank came over and we travelled to a garden centre for plants and a cup of coffee. Later that day I was to travel to Bernard's for tea. This would be an eventful day socially, a time to take my mind off things. I hadn't slept well the previous night through worry over the outcome of the initial investigation. It troubled me that, in spite of an absence of corroborative evidence in support of Alex's story, I sensed, owing to the passage of time, that the police believed his account over mine for reasons of presupposition. I suppose it was the controversial point when the detective had asked the question about the appropriateness of me hugging a lad not related to me, and the fact that in the past I had occasionally allowed lads to sleep at my home.

I had felt my case had been continually judged by today's standards of child protection and safe-caring practice. This left them with a dilemma, of course, which had been to set Alex's accusation against the context of no other hint of sexual impropriety towards youngsters from other records and checks. On one level, arguably, the police had no case to put before a court, but then that did not entirely satisfy me should the matter be closed through a 'lack of evidence'. This had been because my integrity would still have been at stake owing to *even one allegation levelled against me*, for whatever reason. And short of Alex withdrawing his statement — which was inconceivable — I still felt that clouds would always hang over my head. It would be the 'balance of probabilities' that would be the final criteria for social workers and other professionals to arrive at a judgement, not whether there was sufficient evidence to secure a conviction. The dark clouds were the growing uncertainty and secretly held suspicion that I had imagined social workers had had over my involvement with young people.

In a sense there had been indications throughout the interview that suggested to me that whilst the police had been prepared to let me talk away and present my life in brief (outlining a context for supporting young people), with copious illustrations of my lifestyle, when they had arrived at the nitty-gritty details of the accusation, particularly in the manner in which it had been skated over so quickly, I was still left with the feeling that at heart they had felt his story was at least as credible as mine, as credible in fact that I still anticipated being charged at the end of August, my bailed date to attend the station.

There would still remain Alex's claim against my denial, with no corroborative evidence on either side — *how indeed can I negate something never having taken place?* Against the odds, I still felt that they would charge me to be on the safe side. *What was it that was making me feel so anxious when so many 'experts', like Allen, were so certain the case would be closed and thrown out in good time? It was due to the fact, I think, that social workers always appear to operate from a belief that 99.9 per cent of allegations of a sexual nature made against an adult are likely to be correct, and that further it would appear illogical, in their eyes, that Alex would make up such an accusation if it had not contained a kernel of truth. Whilst I may have considered there was a compensation claim at the root of it all, someone else to blame for a lack of sexual competence, or a harboured grudge for being denied further visits to my home 16 years ago, from the point of view of the police it seemed to be irrational that one young man, who had claimed to have 'liked me' and be still 'be very fond of me', would make such an accusation against someone highly respected.*

The discussion I had had with Malcolm the night before ratified this view when he had said that when convicted criminals for vehicle theft and heroin misuse walk into a police station to accuse another it would be against their natural inclination. Normally they keep well way from such places, since for them it represents a betrayal in cooperating with 'the enemy'. So whilst Malcolm and his partner might judge money to be the real motive, and that Alex may have had someone else putting him up to it, for myself there had been that niggling doubt that Alex was operating from a belief that something had actually happened between us, something judged by him later on to be offensive—conveniently not apparent to him before the argument with his girlfriend. My disputation was not so much a 'loss in memory' but a total lack of comprehension.

The doubts and anxieties that had swirled within my mind like a whirlpool sucking me downward into the abyss had left me with that horrible feeling that I no longer wanted to live. Life had become bleak again. *What was the point of going on?*

Shortly afterwards, Sophie sent me the following email, which contained questions posed to assist me to redirect a future beyond school. There was also a religious question she had raised at our last meeting:

Hello Rich,

> Thank you for coming over today. It is good to see your morale increasing. Keep making notes. Use your friends . . . Research all options, but remember you often already have the answer in your own backyard. Note to self: grown men your age also play with old cars. You don't need kids. And as long as you don't mind them rumbling on and on about thromdibulators and scrux screws and exhausts (which you won't) then you can have a good time. Personally I can't think of anything worse and I am sorry but there

is no way gardening is comparable with cars. Gardening is really interesting. Cars aren't. See you the week after next.

Remember too: dine out on all this attention for as long as you can. Why shouldn't all these people give you a bit of love for a change, you deserve a bit of nice after all the rubbish you put up with.

xxx

Sophie

Ps Please work out an answer to the question 'Why do you think God is doing this to you, wasn't the broken back bad enough?' Ask Him next time you speak to Him and see what he says.

I had felt that this much bigger question needed time and reflection to answer.

Going out with Bernard and Frank set my mind on a different line of thought. Although I had felt somehow compelled to keep telling my story for each and every new audience, it had become monotonous to the extent that I was not sure everyone really wanted to hear me as much as I wanted to tell them—I am grateful my friends were not gossipers or busybodies feeling the need to relish in futile tittle-tattle. Attempting to understand the motives of Alex—and fantasising over his motives for having made the accusation—had become pointless and possibly erroneous. I would never know, and as Bernard had said,

"Why do you feel you need to know? That's for others to examine." Frank opened a letter before we went out and it was a formal correspondence from my solicitor summarising my visit to the police station and confirming the bail conditions. Although it was prosaic and factual, it was not pleasant reading an account of the nature of the assault in such lurid detail.

Both Frank and Bernard, in different ways, had begun to speak of their personal unease in never having pointed out more directly the safeguarding risks I had been taking, inadvertently, by teaching lads practical skills over recent years, particularly when engaging with challenging youngsters at my home. In reply, I said that as an adult I did not hold other people responsible for my vocational lifestyle, a manner of living which had proved in general of mutual benefit — I had obviously been naïve in the past over a potential risk with a few cases, but on the whole I had felt I was a good judge of character.

It became evident that I would have to change routine activities whatever the outcome of this case. I had been bruised and there was little point in re-entering the ring a second time. I had a telephone conversation with Jen from Edinburgh that evening and she discussed with me my need to use the opportunity to think afresh my life from this point onward, particularly in regard to retirement and the closing down of my involvement with young people. Jen also offered me a holiday in Tuscany, an invitation I was to take up even though I could not bear hot weather — I thought it would give me a break.

I completed my journal of monotonous recapitulation before retiring to bed, though speculating on how the police would deal with the matter was getting me nowhere. The facts remained that they had to do their job and there was nothing I could do to alter the outcome. I had to face the prospect of acquittal or going to court, of returning to school after their enquiries or packing in, and I could not influence the outcome one iota. *I may well have been charged with sexual assault and have to appear in court in six to nine months time, or I might be freed of my bail conditions, having no case to answer. It was time to disengage from mental rumination and fruitless thought.* From that point on, I pondered whether I should only make descriptive notes of significant changes to my situation.

Just when I decided to refocus my perspective, a telephone call from Patrick's mother raised fresh anxieties. Patrick was required for interview a second time but this time by visiting the local area office of social services, and this time with his mother. It seemed that the previous questioning had not fully examined the two holidays we'd spent together. Patrick's mother later told me that she had been asked whether she had visited my home and inspected the sleeping arrangements when Patrick had stayed whilst on bail at my address. She had said in reply that she felt it would be impertinent and unnecessary to inspect the bedrooms in light of the trust she had had in me. The knot appeared to be pulling tighter together.

Patrick had further told his mother of a strained conversation he had had with an ancillary worker at school, and his mother had wondered whether some staff had discovered that an allegation had been made against me. He was asked where he was living and when he replied 'at his sister's home' she had replied:

"Oh that'll be better than where you were before!" Patrick was put out by the answer and didn't know how to respond. He was going to challenge her over the comment the following day by asking what she'd meant.

I was not sure whether I should have raised the issue with the overseeing social worker or my headteacher because it suggested that rumours had begun to circulate, which would hardly have been surprising. The problem was that for me to have raised it as an issue might suggest that Patrick and me had been in regular communication. It did appear that for me to go back to school was becoming increasingly unlikely. I had found it stressful that the enquiry to date, particularly through social services, had begun not as 'open-ended' and neutral but as prejudicial against me. It had appeared as though they had to search and search for some snippets of information in light of the 'probability' (not 'possibility') that the police would come up with no evidence to press charges and secure a conviction, and that, at the very least in the forthcoming Person in Positions of Trust (PPOT) multi-agency strategy meeting,[7] they might feel compelled to put pressure on the police by 'over-stressing' the concerns they had had over the irregularities they believed were coming to the surface. This raised again for me the complete disregard of everything I had done for teenagers.

I collected my lawnmower from repair that morning and then went to Mary's for light lunch. She asked how I was feeling and I shared new concerns I had had arising from Patrick's telephone call the previous evening. She suggested that casual statements like those are open to misinterpretation, and I said how much it would be better if I could forget the whole thing and await the final decision.

She told me that she had listened to a programme on police targets which said that there were some offences the police took less seriously in order to reach the required quotas. She further said that for a police target to be met it had not been a case of charging, or of satisfactory conviction, but essentially of a case closed. This meant that should the CPS rule 'no case to answer' or, alternatively, that I should be charged, the same target would have been met. I felt this was strangely reassuring, as again I felt that from a logical point of view it wouldn't make sense for me to worry over something of which I had no control.

In British law, I was innocent till proven guilty, and that no matter what the police may have believed, according to Allen, if they had insufficient evidence to bring about a conviction with 80 per cent certainty, then the matter would remain unproven. The case would be closed and I would in status remain innocent simply because there was no evidence to convict. It might be judged therefore as being irrelevant what the police had believed; it was only important what evidence could be found. The police deal not in opinions but essentially in facts. Whatever was going to be the outcome, my adjustment—as a former pupil confidante had said on the first night of the news—in the worst-case scenario of being charged and going to court consisted in asking myself *how bad might that be?*

My pride would have been dented, my job lost, and the opportunity for fresh acquaintances with young people closed. *They might take away my vocation, alter my career, curtail my freedom, but they could not take away the memories, the sense of worthiness I had felt in lightening the burden for many young people — they could not take that away from me.*

After speaking with a friend the previous night and sharing his concerns as well as mine, I had a better night's sleep. I woke up quite refreshed and ready for the long drive to Scotland for my niece's wedding. With my nursing friend Rachel, we drove through splendid mountain scenery through passes I had many fond memories of years ago. I was a little more settled and had thought it was largely because I had felt once again ready to draw a line. It had been, perhaps, something my former headteacher had said when advising that I should 'have a little more faith in myself, in my longstanding reputation and how I was universally respected by professionals and young people'. I would have to sit back and leave the investigating authorities to get on with their work and emotionally cut myself adrift of worry. I could not affect the outcome, and whilst I had suspected that the police would come up with no evidence sufficient enough to warrant charging me from a logical point of view, my gut reaction was that things would not turn out OK, that I would be charged so as to eliminate all risk. I was also sure that social services would have concerns over what they would likely regard as 'irregular practice', concerns which no doubt would be raised at the forthcoming PPOT meeting.

I had been doubtful of finding time to have spoken with Patrick's mother a second time before the following Thursday, and it looked as though they had no one else to question over supposed 'irregularities' in respect of a teacher having young people carry out vehicle maintenance at his home.

The problem for senior social workers was that I had formed stronger bonds with lads like Patrick and Lester than I had ever done with those I had formerly fostered, applying quite different standards as would be expected in fostering, and clearly social services had concerns about this even though the respective lad's parents had given consent and had been approving of my involvement. So whilst they may have had concerns about 'irregular practice', this was not in itself illegal and they therefore had no mandate to dictate how I should choose to live my life in company with youngsters who were not family.

I had been merely practising what I had taught, namely that to change people you have to live with them, walk their walk, and model the type of behaviour to bring ultimate change in order to help them achieve pro-social lives and upward mobility. If social services had a problem with that, then that was their problem.

So let the enquiries go ahead, let them come up with whatever they will, but for myself I will try to become more detached and distracted from what I knew would be happening behind my back, even though it would be horrible to contemplate that a pincer-movement of interrogation was occurring where professionals would be turning over every stone to find whatever was suspected to have taken place in my home 16 years ago.

With the material facts being disputed, corroborative evidence in support of me being an abuser of young people was needed, and with the indisputable fact that literally hundreds of pupils had been supported by me with not the slightest whisper of misconduct or allegation of sexual misconduct or impropriety, I had to rest in the certainty of 'faith in myself' and the testimonies of those who knew me best.

Chapter 10

Weighing the Evidence

It was Tuesday morning in mid July and with the wedding of my niece behind me the days dragged on with little much to do apart from occasional writing. Visits of friends had become less frequent, and having decided to take up the offer of spending two weeks in Tuscany during August with friends from Scotland there was a welcome means of distracting me from endless rumination—each day was a torment, every week an eternity, and returning to work was inconceivable. I needed the break. During my long drive back from Scotland with Rachel I had spoken continually over worries of where the case had been going. In spite of intentions otherwise, I somehow couldn't let events take their course.

We speculated on which homecarers might be called for police interview. I had hoped that any request of a report from a senior homecare manager might bypass a particular practice manager who was renowned for gossip. But then, I had thought, what could a director authoritatively say in writing without consulting the practice manager?

Rachel began to explain how some of the homecare workers initially had been surprised to find school lads in my home, not that they had any suspicions of anything untoward going on, but simply because it wasn't common and due to the fact that I had no female partner at home—*I wonder if every well-meaning bachelor falls under suspicion?* After daily visits, however, they had got to know the lads and myself and were very comfortable with the fact that I had taken an interest in the welfare of delinquent-prone youngsters. They had changed their initial perspectives and had begun to see the mutual benefits of social engagement—a disabled person being helped, and lads learning practical skills of DIY and vehicle maintenance.

In terms of evidence, however, and how events might unfold, I was certain of getting a favourable report from school, from the fostering agency, from my consultant at the spinal unit regarding my physical limitations over the period, from any subsequent interviews with youngsters who had lived with me, such as Patrick, Lester and Malcolm, but I could not be wholly certain of how a report from the homecare service might reflect my manner in relation to the charge of assault against Alex—would they remember him, or even know him?

During these periods of mild depression, my thoughts had centred upon what had been at stake and what I should lose should I be charged, or subsequently be found guilty. One certainty remained, which was that I had never sexually assaulted Alex or hurt him, or anyone else, in any way, yet, I felt, paradoxically, this had hardly been the point. When Jason and Mary popped over one Sunday afternoon, Jason put my mind at ease by suggesting that I should not keep focusing upon my current position; that even if in the worse case scenario that I was found guilty the implications would not be as dire as I might imagine.

I telephoned Gordon and he told me about a judge whom he knew who had spoken of a prominent professional who had been charged for self-masturbation in a public lavatory, simply because the police had reasons to believe that the public convenience was used as a location for soliciting. Particular policemen had actually offered to do the duty of gathering evidence on cameras. *What sort of person,* we both reasoned, *would volunteer for that?* The point he was wishing to make was that certain people had been noticed on camera and of those who were professionals a few had taken their lives when in fact they had done nothing illegal — it was just the shame of publicity.

"That's the way I feel," I said to Gordon, "even though I'm innocent; it's the thought of how I could hold my head up amongst friends and acquaintances — not least my neighbours — should I be charged and found guilty. To be condemned in a court of law is society's way of determining the truth."

Perhaps my ex-headteacher had been right after all when he advised that 'I should have had a little more faith in myself and my reputation and in those who would likely speak up for me.' I was not certain of many things, but one certainty was that if I were to be charged in a few weeks time then my job and place within the school would come to an abrupt and unwholesome end, and not without a small measure of gossip, whether or not I would be acquitted. Should I have been found guilty in a court of law then all that I had achieved in my life since my accident would count as nothing. I would have nothing left apart from the memories, as Sophie had reminded me. The classic cars would have to go; they'd mean nothing to me anymore. My reputation as a writer and public speaker would be shot. All I had achieved would count as nothing.

Being convicted as a Schedule 1 Offender would shadow any public notoriety I think I may have had. Any future employment in counselling would have become unrealistic, since I would be disqualified by my professional body and publicised as dishonourable.

I cannot imagine how my neighbours would view me should the press report a court case, as it probably would do. I would be left as a pathetic disabled man spending his last tiresome and monotonous days being looked after by teams of homecare workers, and a few friends who might just pop in occasionally. When I weighed up these costs, it seemed inconceivable that 'one 29-year-old man' could destroy another person so indefensibly through a fabricated allegation.

I had a terrible night's sleep because Malcolm had telephoned the previous evening and told me that the police had made contact. He told them that he was able to confirm that for eight years he had lived with me, and that these had been the happiest times of his life. I felt proud to have heard what he had said, but a little dismayed after he had told the police that I had been in contact with him. He said that I had informed him that the police might telephone him. He offered to make a full statement if it was required, but the officer said that 'it would probably not be necessary'. So, although I had felt as though things had been moving, that the officers were on the case, I was somewhat dismayed that it appeared as though his evidence would not be entirely relevant, particularly in view of the fact that they knew I had contacted him previous to their call — *obviously, they may have reasoned that I had had an opportunity to influence a potential witness!*

Towards the end of the fifth week I had become more philosophical about my situation, thinking I could do nothing about my plight and would just have to sit it out and bide time. Over that week nothing had happened and fewer friends had called or made contact — it had been pretty boring. My highlight had been the previous day when Patrick rang to share how well his work experience had gone, and the very sound of his voice had left me feeling temporally elated and hopeful of a brighter tomorrow. He told me he had met Chris who had said to him that he had been riding his bike, but did not go very far. They both had said to each other how much they had missed me, and this made me feel briefly proud and valued again.

I was hoping to have spoken with Lester when he arrived home that day to see whether the police had made contact with him, but as was becoming his custom he did not return till very late. I had not been able to communicate with him at all that week, since he was growing up, becoming autonomous, and beginning to fly the nest. It made me feel increasingly lonely; it had not been a good week.

I think the reason why I couldn't sleep that night was because I kept feeling that Graham would have been 'the crucial witness'. What would Graham have said to the police should he have been called in for an interview? I really had no idea, but it seemed as though he would be the most significant person to determine my fate because he had lived at home during the period of Alex's visits. I tried to make contact through telephoning his aunt but then mused over why she had never answered my calls left on the answer-phone. She said in a previous conversation that she had lost touch with him and his brother, and hadn't heard for nearly a year from either of them. I had no idea what he would recall of Alex.

He had often stayed out with friends when Alex paid a visit. He may not have anything significant to tell the police anyway. He would clearly have registered Alex and his brother coming on occasions, but apart from that there was nothing materially he could contribute. Graham was undergoing that independent phase of late adolescence when they become full of themselves and have no particular direction in life but immediate self-interest. All he seemed to want to do, as I recall, was to visit friends and play football; there was no wish to get a job or build a career. I'd heard he'd spent a brief period in prison. Graham would support, I suspect, many of the incidental details of my statement, but apart from that I had no idea what he would or could say. He probably wouldn't want to get involved. *I couldn't imagine he would have any personal grudge against me, but then 16 years had passed; who knows how people change; who knows what reflections he has of the past; who knows what recollections he has over Alex and me?*

Derek, my former student, had raised my anxiety when cautioning me to think twice before contacting ex-students who had offended for support if my case ever went to court:

'They have moved on, mixed in dubious circles some of them, and if any might sniff an opportunity to make money at your expense you have no idea of what they might do or say in court' — so much for my naïvety!

I was expecting a call from my headteacher the previous evening, and there was one call that I had missed. *If this was his call giving me feedback on the second PPOT strategy meeting, then it was perhaps the most important call for me to have taken. In that call I might have learned from him how the case was proceeding.*

I think this was the information I had nervously awaited, and which caused my restless sleep during the early hours. I would have to wait patiently for Daniel to make contact. The message I would dearly have loved to have heard was: 'the police and social workers have now interviewed everyone, and it looks as though the case is going to be dropped'.

I had a surprise visit from the investigating DC the next morning. He wanted signatures to request information from my consultant at the spinal injury unit and my general practitioner. Seizing the opportunity, I asked him whether he would like me to illustrate my practical limitations around the home. He was keen for me to demonstrate the precise level of my disability. I showed him how difficult it was for me to stand and sit, to walk upstairs, and to get into and rise from bed, to turn over my body and to get up in the morning without assistance. He commented that his father had had a stroke and that he was wondering how I avoided pressure sores, and I showed him how I could just about turn my body whist lying on my side. He also asked me whether this was the same bed as I had slept in 16 years ago. I said yes.

He was particularly interested in the tailboard, which, in light of me being so tall, would prevent me from sliding down the bed—I had no detailed knowledge of what Alex had said in his statement, and over which the DC was looking for evidence, and so could only answer questions put directly to me without drawing any inference. Apparently, the tailboard was very significant to the charge Alex had made. Finally, after descending from the stairs, I went into the kitchen and showed him exactly how Alex had been received by me six months previous to the allegation.

I gave him a copy of a book I had written on coping with disability, together with my care plan. He said that he wished to talk to my regular carer, and I gave him her mobile number. I said that I was very happy for him to be present while she got me up in the morning so that he could view firsthand her administrations and my handicap. I asked him about Graham and my other lodgers in the house at the time and he told me that he had not as yet spoken with anyone else. I took the opportunity to explain why I had felt it was necessary to forewarn Malcolm that he would be calling him.

"Being an ex-offender, I could not be sure whether Malcolm would react aggressively to a cold call from a police detective." He seemed satisfied with my explanation, and had been quite reassuring in some ways. I had felt, from his manner and reactions, that this visit had achieved much in terms of supportive evidence for my case. Perhaps I had been worrying too much, but then again I still thought it would all depend on what Graham or my lodgers might have to say. If they had made little comment of significance, I felt I would have been cleared, and cleared quite quickly. But then there might have been evidence arising from the medical records, which, I estimated, would take some time to process and come through.

The officer visited the following Friday to return my care plan document after taking a photocopy, and whilst there he took the opportunity to interview my regular homecarer. They had spoken together for quite some time, about three quarters of an hour, as I recall, and she made a statement and gave consent that she would be willing to attend court if required to be a witness. This surprised me, and again illustrated that I was a long way from being cleared.

Before leaving, I asked him if he would like to see the room where Alex had occasionally slept. He acknowledged and followed me around the house. He made mental notes but asked no particular question of significance.

My homecarer later told me that she had been asked about the nature of my disability, and she confirmed that I could raise my arms barely to shoulder height, and that when lying down I could hardly move at all. She said that if my head settled low down to the side of my pillow, I would say the next morning that I had found it uncomfortable and that I could not move the pillows unaided. I began to muse on his interest in the tailboard of my bed, and it had all seemed to be moving in a positive direction, which was to endorse the degree of my physical limitations to do as Alex had alleged.

Maybe I had been worrying too much; maybe it was a closed case. I wished I could let go and be content to let things take their course. It had dawned on me early one Saturday morning that two highly significant events had taken place, events that had involved the police detective visiting my home. These two visits had settled my mind, somewhat, at least temporarily, but still the nagging worry would not go away. The following night, for example, in the early hours, I had searched the Internet for possible sentences that a convicted person might receive for indecent assault. *Why on earth did I do this?*

I guess my low spirit was due to loneliness. I had seen few people that week, apart from Jason and Mary one evening, and two former teacher colleagues who happened to call in for 15 minutes on the previous day. I completed my journal and felt the case would not turn out the way I had wanted, in spite of my friends being unanimously of the opinion that it simply could go nowhere. I never found out whether the police interviewed, or had any intention of interviewing, Graham or my lodgers over Alex visiting my home 16 years ago.

Chapter 11

Temporary Relief

Daniel called me on the phone on Thursday evening of the sixth week to give feedback from the multi-agency PPOT meeting. He had commented favourably upon the investigating DC and the discussion he had had with him regarding the Principal Officer of Allegations against Professionals. This person had become my most vocal opponent. She held a powerful, strategic post in the authority, and was the officer responsible for managing child protection accusations against local authority employees. My future integrity was to be held in question and I was to suffer heavily under her self-portrayed guise of being the only person dedicated to protecting children against the wiles of predatory professionals ('like me!') in positions of trust. On leaving the second PPOT meeting, and after hearing her deliberations, DC Henderson said to my headteacher:

"Mm, guilty before proved innocent!" Daniel didn't comment, but later shared with me further detail that, perhaps, he should not have done so, which was that social services had interviewed Patrick, but 'got nowhere'.

"It seems as though social services can find no 'evidence' of anyone having concerns about you. This is going nowhere." In reply I said that the only matter to resolve if the police clear me was my employment status, and what changes I might have to make when returning to work, detail I had already discussed with him. He also said that the police were not meant to 'go fishing around' for information at this stage of an enquiry, and that from his understanding of legal procedures they would not be required to interview people like Graham.

"I'm surprise about that—he would surely be a material witness. Both Alex and I have mentioned him. He would be able to confirm or deny details of our various accounts. He would be the most important witness, surely?" Although I couldn't be sure whether Alex had claimed that Graham was present during the alleged event, he was certainly around and would have a view on our relationship. The investigating DC, when in my home, had also intimated that he might not have cause to speak with Graham. *Could I suppose the DC was on my side after all and not really wanting it to go much further, that he merely had a job to do to find evidence and to check the details I had given him were correct?*

Whilst composing my notes, I received a call from Derek, my former student, and we spoke at length about the police in general.

"You must remember", he said, "that in order to do their job they have no feelings at all, otherwise they couldn't do what they do. They have to look at the evidence dispassionately, and it doesn't matter what they think—If you're guilty or innocent. They're only concerned with charging you if they can prove offences have occurred. In other words, don't get carried away with thinking the police have feelings either way." *I wish I could find out whether the police have a view on who is really telling the truth, on whether they are trained to discard intuition, feelings and gut-reaction in place of following the evidence dispassionately. I'll ring Allen when he returns from holiday.*

From the last week in July to the first in August I took an opportunity for a holiday in Tuscany with my friends, Jen and Paul. They had a second home in a quaint Tuscan village, high up in the hills of Western Italy, and frequently visited there during the summer break. At first I declined, saying to my friend Jen that I didn't think I would be very good company, feeling the need, as I did, to keep chewing over my current troubles. And in addition, I added, I didn't think the hot climate would suit me. I'd often envied friends who had visited Tuscany and on balance would have preferred to have gone in the spring or autumn, but having this opportunity and since they were passing my front door en route anyway it seemed foolish to let the opportunity go.

"I don't know why I don't bite your hand off considering."

"Then why don't you while it's being offered," she replied. In due course, I considered the matter and took up their offer. This was a welcomed break, and whilst I discussed fairly often my narrative of despair, the holiday had proved to be a diversion from wallowing in self-pity.

On my return, I was keen to know how Patrick had viewed his second interview with social workers, and after telephoning his mother she confirmed that the interview had gone quite well and that the family had received a letter thanking them for their time and saying that there were no further concerns since the matter 'had now been closed'. Again, I had felt relieved but wanted to know more about the nature of their conversations. I had wanted to stop being defensive and was looking for an opportunity to attack rather than ever be on the retreat, particularly in regard to social services. But I had realised that until the police had formally closed their enquiries, I was in no position to attack anybody. I had been stuck with the waiting game.

Patrick's mother could not give me any details of the interview, because her younger daughters were in earshot of the telephone, but she promised to ring me later on that day. On hearing further detail, it appeared there had been nothing of any substance to worry about, so mentally I could close my mind on that area of the investigation, a point later confirmed by Daniel from the PPOT meeting.

On the following Wednesday, I telephoned my solicitor to see whether he had done as he had promised he would do and ring the police for an update. He failed to do this, however, and could not even recall promising to do so. He further said that a different solicitor was to take on my case, that he would contact her and that she would ring me to introduce herself. She rang me two days later to say that she had failed to contact the investigating DC, since he had been on two day's holiday leave, but promised to get in touch with him at first opportunity.

She wanted to know a little more detail of the case, and I was happy to brief her. She seemed more determined to fight my corner, I had felt, and I was more impressed with her than with my former solicitor — she was vigilant, more on the ball. She spoke about the role of the police, confirming in a sense what my former student had said. She outlined that the police were there to prosecute me on behalf of the plaintiff, and that I should not get carried away with any illusions about the police being on anybody's side, least of all mine. A policeman's job is to collect sufficient evidence to warrant a case being brought against me so that I could be charged. She further said that in her opinion the bail date at the end of August was unrealistic, that in all likelihood my bail would be extended to allow the police more time to examine the evidence and arrive at a decision.

I became a little disheartened again by the dragging out of my case. She had a holiday booked with a friend and would like to have taken a few days off, which would mean negotiating a date in early September. *How my case seems to drag on; will I ever become free?*

My former headteacher rang me a day later in support and to offer to meet up sometime during the summer break. He gave me encouragement, convinced, as he had always been, that the accusation would amount to nothing. In the back of my mind, however, there had been a sentiment expressed by Sophie when she had said that I was not the only one to be concerned, that those in 'managerial positions' of my employment would also have cause to be worried, worried about their own level of culpability and would follow the outcome of my case with more than a passing interest.

"After all", she added, "if someone in a position like yours, as a counsellor for many years in the same school, having had such dealings both professionally and personally with hundreds of youngsters over a long period, are to be found guilty, then heads would roll in high places. Consider the three heads you've worked under. They were fully aware of your involvement with pupils in and out of school, since you've been so public in supporting teenagers, even in your home. Consider again social services and your contacts with them over the years, working on procedures of child protection policy and attending CP conferences. Then, again, there is the Fostering Service, in placing youngsters under your care. Could you imagine how many heads would roll in positions of power if you were found guilty? No, I cannot see prosecuting you would be in the public interest at all." While I went along with much of what Sophie had said, I did not agree that many former and current colleagues were primed by self-interest and motives of merely 'covering their own backs', but I must admit that it was a fleeting thought at times.

Daniel rang me the following Monday to see if there had been any news and to fill in a few missing details of previous interviews. I briefed him and brought him up to date, and further promised to take him and his wife out to lunch should I be/or when I had been/cleared of the suspicion of assault. He had seemed surprisingly optimistic still and in some ways I gained further momentum to keep positive from our ongoing conversations. But the show would not be over till the fat lady sings, as they say. So, whilst I remained optimistic, there was still that nagging doubt that the police might charge me, and thereby effectively close my counselling career at school.

A school attendance worker debriefed me how a case conference had gone with young Christopher. One contribution highlighted the benefit of the counselling he had received, and this lifted my spirits for further involvement and to glimpse a future opportunity to engage him as my ongoing motor mechanic. However my story was to turn out, there was one thing I had been sure about. One day I would welcome the opportunity to speak with Chris and to have told him the truth about my absence and withdrawal from his life. I had owed him that much.

So, I engaged myself in reading and reading and more reading, whilst hoping and hoping that things might turn out in my favour and that I may have been reinstated. There had been one matter I was absolutely certain about, and that was that if I was to be charged the curtains would finally draw on my role as a school counsellor — nine months, the average length of such legal proceedings, would simply be too long, however the court case turned out.

I hadn't seemed quite as anxious as before I went to Tuscany, and indeed the holiday had done me much good in that respect. I suppose I was becoming resigned to the fact that I could in no way affect my fate. I could only await the decision of the CPS. I had wanted to fight back against the system that had put me through this perpetual torment, but that would only have been possible at some future time, and, I suppose, I was also getting used to living a life with no young people around me. In fact, I hadn't seen a young person or been in company with anyone under 16 for over two months. Since most cases of allegations against teachers last approximately three months, I reasoned I had four weeks to go. I had little contact with teachers and colleagues from school, and perhaps this had not been a bad thing if the cover story was to hold till the opening of the September term.

Frank came over during the week and I guided him in changing inner tubes on his mountain bike. On the Friday I travelled to Sophie's for lunch and took a pleasant trip to a garden centre. All I seemed to be doing was filling in time. *Why oh why did not the telephone ring with the investigating DC telling me the CPS had looked over the case and returned a verdict that I had no case to answer?*

Over mid-August floods occurred in the north and south of England, and on one Saturday it had rained continually. I felt bored, with no chores or jobs to do. I wanted the heavy rain clouds to lift and the sunshine to beam through with a promise of a brighter tomorrow. I reflected on the support of my friends, but I realised that they had been, inevitably, 'telling me what I had wanted to hear'. The significant folk were to be the police and the CPS.

How would they view Alex? What sense would they make of his statement? Was he a Judas, the betrayer of Jesus, or a Galileo standing up for truth? Has he betrayed a friend for some unknown cause? Or has he taken a moral stand? What are the facts? I rehearsed them once again:

➢ Sixteen years ago Alex had chosen to support me, a disabled person. We had become friends. I got to know his family well and invited him into my home at times to ease the tension of quarrelling with his brother — a relationship his mother, often depressed, found difficult to manage.

➢ He occasionally stayed overnight and once went with me on holiday to Scotland where we stayed with two family friends.

➢ Other lads in time took over the role of my support because I had felt our friendship had outlived itself in that he was investing too much in me and too little in his own family. I, in consequence, stopped him coming to my home.

> He went to prison after leaving school through car theft and heroin misuse.

> During those occasions of imprisonment, he would have had access to a welfare department and a probation officer, who would in turn have offered therapeutic support over causes and remedies of criminality and drug-abusive behaviour.

> For some reason, 'should he have been abused by a teacher-counsellor in youth', he elected to say *absolutely nothing*, to keep his mouth shut (from my perspective because 'nothing happened', but from his who knows?).

> He had visited me twice after leaving school — once to try and sell me an old bench lathe, another, six months before making the allegation, to re-acquaint himself and to tell me he had now settled and had been living near my home.

> Now, being free of those past misdeeds, and having had a partner and young child, he had seen fit to accuse me of an obscenity against him, which potentially ceased my therapeutic support of youngsters in school, leaving young Christopher friendless and Patrick without his mentor, myself out of a job, and my reputation shot.

What had he to gain by making the allegation? I simply had no idea, save for the possibility of compensation for 'having been injured through youth' — a motive that would have been impossible to prove, since it's always in retrospect of criminal proceedings having been completed that so-called 'injured parties' file for compensation. Since he was not the person under investigation, this as a plausible motive would have been impossible to prove and therefore in my case was largely irrelevant.

Now just suppose he had been abused by me at the age of 13, believing that something had taken place, of which I have no recollection. Let's run with the idea that he had enjoyed sexual encounters whilst under my care, a hypothesis that would appear as credible from revelations of Alex's statement the police had (surprisingly) revealed to me during the interview.

> ➤ He had claimed that he had been having difficulty in performing sexually with his girlfriend, and this had led to bitter disagreements between them.
> ➤ In defending his case, he had claimed to his girlfriend that the reason he was sexually impotent or malfunctioning was because his father together with a teacher later on had assaulted him.

Sophie's conjecture was that this was a typical 'copout' of some men in an age that refuses to apportion self-responsibility. But then, the police should have seen right through this. But for the sake of argument, let's run with it and see where the reasoning takes us, since I don't know which way they might have been thinking. Let's assume that they would be going along with his version and reason from such a perspective.

> ➤ Alex had visited me (both accounts agree) six months before the allegation was made. What on earth was the point of that visit? Ostensibly, it had been to renew our

friendship after a long period of no contact, and to say that he was 'doing well' and 'keeping out of trouble', with the additional pledge to 'keep in touch'.

➤ Since, according to his account, he had 'chosen' to visit me at home, in spite of a past 'assault', then how could it be argued that such a visit is consistent with behaviour of one who has been 'offended' in youth? The point is that his behaviour is untypical of that of an abused victim.

➤ Supposing I had assaulted him, why indeed would he have not blown the whistle to his mother, his brother, or to any authority, either at the time, just afterwards when it could be reasoned he had cause to be bitter, or later on whilst in prison?

➤ Should this not argue — again from the police officers' perspectives — that he had not been 'injured' at all, or 'assaulted', but had actually enjoyed it, that he was a consenting accomplice, as he had said to the police, 'I was aroused by what had happened'? Then if this was the case, why did he betray me by going to the police — make a complaint over something he had initiated with a severely disabled person? Was it because 'he didn't realise that what was supposed to have taken place was 'abusive' till later on, till experiencing sexual impotence with his girlfriend? For God's sake he's 30; he's not a kid anymore, but an adult!

➤ Could it have been that the point of the visit was to 'clear up' the confusions of what had supposedly taken place 16 years ago, at least in his own mind, or might it be feasible to suggest that he might have wanted continued sexual relations with me, presupposing I might have been gay (factually inaccurate), and him being 'still' attracted to me?

This last notion I found offensive and personally degrading. If the police were following this line of reasoning, that would put him more in line as a 'betrayer' of one of whom he was still fond, and again, according to his account, one for whom he still had strong feelings. This would make him a Judas, rather than a Galileo.

This circular line of reasoning was getting me nowhere. Was Alex a fully functioning, rational person, I had wondered? Has his brain been scrambled through heroin misuse? Or was his deed simply an ill-thought-out, impromptu deed to save face with his girlfriend? Either way, he has potentially destroyed my life and cast a cloud over my integrity and reputation, and, yet, I suspect he has not the slightest idea of what he has put me through.

Chapter 12

Expanding the Confidence Circle

It had been the beginning of my ninth week of torture. Over the weekend I organised a family barbecue, an annual event I arrange with cousins on my father's side of the family. Although it poured down with rain it was good to see everybody once again. I had spoken with my cousin from Yorkshire and shared only with him my current dilemma. He was sympathetic and reassuring. Our discussion was cut short owing to the arrival of younger members of the family, where it would not have been appropriate to share such matters. In consequence, he rang the next day and pledged his full support and shared with me his concerns over the type of culture that was inadvertently being shaped by current child protection policy and litigation. I took the opportunity to give him the full account. He discussed with me his own take on the social consequences over the apparent ease by which accusations are made today against professional people.

He described a recent incident when walking past some young children and smiling whilst they were engaged in play, at which point their mother gave a suspicious glance and pulled her children away as though they were in threat of imminent attack from a paedophile. He also went on to describe a group of Croatian men who had felt incriminated when offering sweets to young children. Professional people had advised them not to do this, but they protested and said it comes as natural to us; from where we come from all men give children sweets.

"We give children sweets at home, why shouldn't we do the same here?" This highlighted the social implications of unfounded allegation cases like mine.

After giving an outline of the accusation and my current situation, my cousin made two points. First, he said that he was prepared to offer me any support I was in need of, including accompanying me during any formal meeting. Second, he said that I must commit my thoughts and feelings to writing.

"It is imperative," he said, "that you record all this, because your story has massive implications for a good many other professional people. And also your experience would serve as an alarm to where the current false-allegation-compensation-culture was leading regarding the withdrawal of voluntary service through a heightened nervousness to become involved with young people and vulnerable adults – the invisible cost for society. We seem to be moving towards people not getting involved with children and teenagers because of overzealous procedures and health and safety legislation surrounding child protection." We both recognised the need to protect children, and to be vigilant in this area, but if over-cautious restrictions and excessively risk-aversive obstacles leave us with the kind of society where all professionals and charitable services do just the minimum of superficial engagement in order to 'cover their backs', then society will end up the poorer.

Although he also had been doubtful my case would go very far, I shared with him that I suspected they would charge me, a belief founded on two factors. First, I considered that Alex had given an account to the police which appeared to be coherent if unusual and untypical of that of an abused victim, and one which had eliminated, initially at least, one primary objective, that of compensation. Second, given that I had been such a popular person and practitioner of repute, both amongst professionals and with troublesome youths, together with their families, it would have appeared strange for the police that given these factors Alex was still prepared to cross the threshold and make an allegation of indecent assault against me — mine was indeed a big scalp to take.

The problem for the police in weighing up the evidence over whom to believe had been whether they could find sufficient evidence to support his case and prosecute me or to invalidate his claim through contradicting factors and send him on his way. My solicitor had left me in no doubt where the police would be coming from, and that I should not get carried away with any dreamy-eyed notion that they may be on my side. They would either drop the case or be seeking evidence to prosecute me. She was painting the blackest of all pictures.

It had become the social implications of my case that had become the focus of my growing concerns. This had been observed by my cousin who recommended that I should record everything in writing, and not wait for two years after the event before doing so. If the net result of prosecuting me would mean that all teachers and professionals, youth leaders, including church folk known to me, would become even more reluctant to get involved with needy youngsters, then this could not be a positive direction for society; it would leave demoralised and discouraged all those engaged in creating socially cohesive communities.

So, the question had become whether it was 'in the public interest' to charge me and risk an acquittal in court, or to 'militate against increased paranoia towards professionals supporting the disadvantaged' by releasing me of bail conditions and ruling 'no case to answer' through a lack of corroborative evidence. Little did I know at the time that social services would have a different view on the matter?

There was only one week left before the final decision, yet, curiously, I became less stressed over whether or not I would be charged, even though I knew that being charged would close my door of work at school. My only regret was that being charged would effectively cease any engagement with Chris; that would come to an untimely end. I couldn't support him through adolescence towards adulthood or have his help in maintaining my classic cars. Patrick would be left without his mentor to carry him through those final stages of independence and to help build non-violent relationships.

I lay awake in the early hours that night with a nagging anticipation of being charged. In a sense, I had persuaded myself that 'positive thinking' required me to view this as the probable outcome. I had prepared myself like a young person would a driving test, announcing to his friends and convincing himself that in all likelihood he would fail, but then if he had passed then this would come as a pleasant surprise. Paradoxically, it seemed more comforting to think this way; to be overly pessimistic that the sequel would not be what I had wanted to happen. I sat by the phone anxiously waiting for the investigating officer to give me an answer of reprieve.

Later that morning, I met up with two friends, Peter and Frank, for a meal in a country pub. This was a regular occurrence for retired friends, at least the men of our acquaintance, and since I was now in a position of semi-retirement I had been welcomed into the group. Bernard had previously commented in humour,

"I'm amazed at what lengths you have gone to to get into our retirement lunch party!" Whilst sitting at the table over haddock and chips, we engaged in the regular discourse of 'grumbling old men', lamenting the passing of former times when life seemed so simple, uncomplicated and, apparently, more dictated by values. All in the group, in various ways, had spent endless hours in youth work and we recounted all the fun we had had in a much freer and less-restricted time.

I talked of the times I had taken lads to Snowdonia, and of the joviality shared through sleeping in the same army ridge tent. The camaraderie was spontaneous and all because the lads, my fellow teacher and myself, were all in the same tent — all decent, no malpractice, no deviancy and no suspicion. I had emphasised the point by reiterating how this regular outward-bound trek had ceased at the point at which a union rep at school had cautioned that we should 'not have slept in the same tent as the pupils'. That ended our visits to Snowdon. Sadly, it was no longer feasible to plan the same trip owing to the cost and logistics of having to take an extra tent in a space-restricted minibus.

All my acquaintances — in teaching, the church and in youth work — could tell similar stories of obstacles arising from 'health and safety', 'safe-caring practice' and 'minimising risks of allegations' through having restrictive child protection protocols, that had effectively stopped or seriously curtailed their involvement with young people.

"Our society is currently suffering from paranoia, hyped up by the media, that there's a paedophile at the end of every street, and responsible parents have little option but to keep an ever-watchful eye over their youngsters at play", I had said. I can remember during my own youth that I was similarly warned about 'not getting into cars with strangers', 'not receiving money from folk I didn't know' and to 'play near the house', but there was not that paranoid anxiety that danger was lurking around every corner that I sense is the case in Britain today. Frank had said that at his church they could no longer get members prepared to run the youth club, and Peter had said that over the radio there was a national shortage of youth clubs to engage young people and of youth leaders who were willing to do the job. Why was I not surprised?

Now, I do recognise that social workers do a thankless job and receive little recognition of the many things they get right, that they receive undue criticism and public remonstration on those odd occasions when things go wrong, and I am not wishing to advocate that we relax our hold on the tiller with regard to child protection, but I am saying that we should see what sort of society we are inadvertently shaping by unsympathetic, unnecessarily lengthy and strictly adversarial procedures brought into operation with every unfounded allegation against a teacher or professional worker 'without evidence'.

I am certainly not saying that my case should have been handled in-house, and in any other way than with complete transparency, but what I am really pleading for is that the authorities should deal with all dubious Section 47 Enquiries in a more efficient and time-limited way — three months is too long to put innocent people through the mill, particularly when enquiries are likely to lead nowhere.

The problem is one of investigating officers being pushed to 'cover their backs', in my opinion, where a principal concern is for professionals wishing to militate against their own culpability should procedures not be followed.

Children can be manipulative and ulterior motives can lie behind an individual making a disclosure. Not often, but it does occur. At least, this has been my experience, and the experience of some teachers and foster parents I know who have undergone an investigation. However, I find that designated social workers and child protection officers are a breed apart in that they function universally as though children 'always tell the truth' and adults 'often lie' to cover up. The truth is never as simple as that.

My central point is that once we lose the goodwill to support unfortunate youngsters voluntarily (and at personal cost) of those having a commitment, or, dare I say, vocation, for such work, it will not return. Child protection protocols have become far too cumbersome and incriminating for those who are innocent but no politician would risk political capital by reforming them: *once toothpaste is squeezed from the tube you can't get it back in again.*

I rang my solicitor to see whether my bailed date at the police station was realistic for the CPS to have arrived at their decision. Being unavailable, I left a message. She rang me back later that morning to say that she had been in touch with the investigating officer, who had said that we would have to move the bail date to the middle of September, owing to the fact that he was still awaiting a report from my consultant at the spinal injury unit. My heart sank. I was disheartened to think that we were waiting still for documents to come through, but at least, I had thought, it had removed from my mind that nagging fear that I was likely to be charged because I had heard nothing to the contrary.

I was invited to dinner at Jason and Mary's that day, and on my return there was a message from the investigating officer on my answer-phone explaining his frustrated attempts to get the full medical report. I telephoned him the next day and he explained that the consultant was now back from holiday, that he had faxed a single sheet providing a brief report on my condition but that it was too superficial and lacked detail, and that they would get from him a fuller report when he could find the time. DC Henderson asked my consultant's secretary to specify a date by which he could 'expect to receive the full report'.

I later telephoned my headteacher to discuss with him whether we should not now have a change in plan. Given that I was not likely to return to school till the second or third week in September, at the earliest, should we not, I suggested, tell a small number of principal staff the reason I was absent from school.

"Perhaps," I said, "if we stressed the sensitivity of my situation by not speaking more broadly to others of what had happened, then this might allay rumours." He was strongly of the opinion that we should stick to the same script, that of letting colleagues and pupils think that I was still unwell.

"After all, given your condition, it's not likely to draw much attention as might be the case if you were a healthy teacher," he said. I conceded and allowed him to handle the matter his way. Some staff have occasionally been unprofessional and passed on confidential information with elder pupils, but in my case this never occurred. I was aware, and so was my headteacher at this point, that we had to plan some damage limitation. He said that he would discuss the matter with a senior colleague so as not to jeopardise any chance of me ever returning to school as the counsellor.

My mood increasingly became a little more positive at this time because I had a reason for the police not to have made earlier contact, that indeed the officer was awaiting the final report before the CPS could arrive at decision. I had wondered whether the report would give them the required information, whether it might be over-technical or have provided insufficient detail of my physical disabilities over the period to serve as material evidence to negate the claim of indecent assault. What might the report say, for example, of my ability to force a physical act against the will of a teenager?

How could it confirm or refute particular claims that Alex had made of our engagement? Only time would tell.

It was weird how my state of limbo had caused me to flit from being negative to positive, then back to being negative again. How my mind had oscillated with every fantasy formed from new information. My feelings rolled from hope to despair and in spite of being a professional therapist I had been unable to control my emotions through mental regulation; only with the words of support from friends could I harness a restless spirit. New, or lack of, information over the period had caused doubt to grow like a weed taking hold in crazy paving.

Whilst being in this melancholy mood, Patrick rang to say that he had been at a loss and had nothing to do. It cheered me to hear his voice and I was keen to share our various stories since last we met. There had been a lot of catching up to do, but I didn't want to speak on the phone.

We were both facing the possibility of going to court, and of prosecution. I had an ally in Patrick, and he in me, but how on earth could we help each other was not clear to see at this point.

I spent that afternoon with Rachel supporting Lester in practising his wedding speech for his sister's wedding. This was the day he was to give his sister away in marriage to her partner. He had cleaned the old Rover and looked smart in his new suit and waistcoat, asking my neighbour and brother how he should tie a cravat. I was quite impressed with Lester because I knew he would be nervous about the speech, but he appeared quite confident.

Later that afternoon, Patrick rang me to say he was coming over. It was so nice to see him and we exchanged each other's news. He told me that this had not been a good summer holiday for him, and I sympathised and said the same applied to me. I felt cheered to spend a few hours with him, although he was very tired — having spent a late night at his cousin's house watching late-night movies. I explained to him that I had cause to be a little more optimistic than in former weeks, but that I could not be sure at this point what would be the outcome even though the latest signs looked promising.

I pledged that I would be prepared for him to come back if this was his wish, and he said it clearly was, and that he could not wait to get back, saying how he had felt unsettled in his sister's home. There had been a clear risk that he was breaking the conditions of his bail, and this would put him in peril should the police check up — he would be put straight back into custody. I said to him that in view of the fact that there were only a few weeks left before his trial he was taking a gamble. He should stick to the rules and not leave himself open. This was imperative because, as his mother had shared with me, those who had pressed charges were looking for an opportunity to move from the area and one claim they may make is that Patrick had threatened a witness. On the way home, I took him to McDonalds for something to eat and he gave me a hug as he left.

I had felt so happy, although I had to check myself because the final decision had not as yet been made: *the show would not be over till the fat lady sings*. It may only be a week or two to hear, apart from the possibility that the CPS may need to subject the report from the spinal unit to their head office if the information was too technical to enable them to arrive at a final decision. I told Patrick there were four hurdles for me to get over.

> ➤ The first was the decision from the CPS. I could make no mental or practical plans until I had received that decision and had jumped the first hurdle.
> ➤ The second was to view how I might accommodate what recommendations social services might make in the event of the police throwing the case out.
> ➤ The third hurdle was coming back to school and facing up to the possible suspicions that were likely to circulate—many no doubt being unspoken. I shared with him the sequence of possible rumours beginning.
> ➤ The final hurdle was to know how to deal with young Christopher. I had said to Patrick that I would be honest with him, but that I would not know how to handle the question of whether or not his aunt and uncle should be informed, or that indeed his social worker should be told of allegations made against me. This may be a technical question because social services would have a database that included details of the accusation made against me. If such information was accessed by his social worker, for Chris to help me after school again could not occur without him sanctioning the matter.

Finally, I told Patrick that I had missed him very much and that I was still very fond of him, but I also said that I was fond of Chris and missed him too. I shared with him that I was low and that I had once considered suicide but that it was the thought of Patrick and little Chris that prevented me from taking my life.

"You may be surprised, but this is how low I felt, far lower than during my spinal injury days in hospital." He said that if I had taken my life then he 'would have been in bits', and that he felt he could not have handled that if it should have occurred.

Both parents had rejected Christopher, but then he had put trust in me. I had to get over the hurdle of whether he'd be able, or allowed, to help me after school and all that that might entail, an issue in need of review with the head when meeting with him and his wife over dinner when the right time had come. But all this had to wait till the sequence had unfolded stage by stage.

I felt my paralysis ever more acutely as I sat and read, or wantonly flicked through television programmes for just one that might hold my interest, often longing for a phone call or a visit from a friend; something to relieve the sheer monotony and boredom. I looked at people passing by from my window and noticed the smiles on their faces but felt unable to afford myself such similar contentment. I found this to be a particularly trying period, I think, in retrospect, far worse than had been that period in the spinal unit.

There were times I had prayed, but let me qualify what I mean by prayer. I have never found praying easy and I'm not sure what I prayed for or to whom I was praying. I have read and studied all the classical arguments for and against God's existence and the efficacy/non-efficacy of prayer, and regarded myself as a spiritual person generally. I have studied all the classical philosophers of the Enlightenment and considered the issues of existentialism and nihilism, but still retain a belief in a numinous Being, that indefinable element of Otherness.

I am not a formal Christian, or churchman. I think institutions are formed by individuals influenced by social factors and for a purpose of collective benefit. Neither am I a polytheist, since most gods are carved within the imaginations of people's minds and cultural experiences, and I think if there is a Spirit of the universe it must be a singular unity of unimaginable (if any) form. I'm not a pantheist either because I think to say that God is in 'everything' is to say that God is in nothing particular, which is meaningless.

No, I think that God is an indefinable mystical element that is only ever-present for those preconditioned to view Him that way. If He or She exists, it is clear that such a Being is not detectable through empirical means and rational thought, but is a reality that runs alongside and yet within the material atoms of the universe in an unfathomable union—I recognise that such a contention is not falsifiable. So, I could not therefore answer Sophie's question until time had passed and I was able to view the sequel and look backwards—could there be meaning and purpose in what I was going through? Who knows?

I suppose I had been praying for a sense of justice to prevail over the accusation made by Alex and that the CPS would return a favourable verdict.

That night I spoke openly with my nightly homecare assistant, and shared with her the stage of the current investigation. I had spoken with her before because she was a foster carer herself and had concerns about the prevalence of accusations against carers. We were discussing the details of Alex's claim, particularly the statement of still being 'fond of me'. She knew that Alex had never actually lived with me, but that he had occasionally stayed some weekends over 16 years ago, that he had made a social visit six months before making the allegation, and that he had told the police that he expressed a wish to keep in more regular contact.

"Why did he go to the police then?" She responded with surprise and a little outrage.

"Now that's a question that has never been pressed?" I asserted.

"How do you feel after knowing that?" She further enquired. I explained to her that after being asked the same question by the police I told them that it had made me feel sick and slightly nervous about what had been the true purpose of his visit. I further said that it must be a mystery to the police as to what Alex's true motives really are, and that in a sense it had made my predicament worse:

"What do you mean?"

"Well, the problem is that it takes away the motive of compensation, when you think about it. Alex comes over to the police, or at least he could come over to the police, as a person who is now an upright citizen who, whilst enjoying the alleged sexual pursuits of our engagement 16 years ago, now presents himself as viewing the past through a different pair of spectacles, not least because he is now the father of a little girl. In claiming that he, as a minor, had enjoyed illicit sexual relations that were supposed to have taken place between us, he now views it as inappropriate through the eyes of a 30-year-old adult. His motive, taking this hypothesis, is to exercise his social conscience to help remove a foster carer who must, according to this speculation, be a regular abuser of young people under his charge."

"I don't really see what you're getting at," she replied.

"Looking at the circumstantial evidence from this perspective, Alex presents a coherent story. Follow the reasoning," I suggested. "He comes to my home and stays overnight occasionally, even travels to Scotland with me on one occasion. 'During the sleeping hours', he claims, 'we engage in sex'. For him, he's merely experimenting with me as his companion. I, as a responsible adult, allow this to take place—I am therefore culpable. It has no sexual excitement for me because I have no neurological sensations in the lower part of my body, and neither am I aroused or drawn to having sex with young boys. But I allow myself to be an instrument for his pleasure and broadened experience. He has no regrets and to all intents and purposes wishes this to continue, but I, on the other hand, begin to see the seriousness of where this behaviour might lead in terms of my own position as a responsible adult foster carer and school counsellor. I begin to see with alarm where this behaviour would lead and decide to terminate our involvement so that it went no further. I tell Alex that I no longer wish him to stay overnight at my home, and he becomes extremely angry, almost at the point of jealous rage, particularly in the light of other boys beginning to help me at school and at home instead of him. Now can you see a possible motive within a coherent narrative should this be presented in a court of law? If the police hold this line of reasoning, then it's possible they might suspect that I am guilty, that I have something to hide and that I am lying to get myself off the hook, which potentially has the effect of destroying me and questioning my integrity. Now can you see what I mean?"

"Bloody hell, I can, but then come on," she continued. "The police are bound to see through that. Surely he would have reported this sort of thing to the police a long time ago if it had happened."

"Yes, you'd think so, but then how might shame and self-guilt cause a person not to disclose to authorities an offence against a popular disabled bloke whom he claims to be still fond of? That is a further quandary the police would have to address with evidence and not merely with supposition or general perceptions on paedophilic behaviour. Why didn't he blow the whistle if this was what had happened 16 years ago? But then why should he do it now?"

Gordon returned my call later that evening after his holiday to see how matters had progressed whilst away. I told him the case was no further forward and that at this point I was awaiting the final decision, still waiting for the report from the spinal injury unit to complete the file. He sympathised once again, recalling his own experience when he had had to wait for over six months to be released of worry. Again, like so many of my friends, he reiterated his belief that my case would not go far.

"Could you imagine how a jury would respond just seeing you turn up in a wheelchair in court? Remember that they will not view Alex as an innocent little boy of 13. They will see him as a 29-year-old who is making a considerably late allegation. Look at your record; look at his. Now, I know what it feels like to have to wait, but when you have your final decision you'll feel a great burden lifted from your shoulders. You will be able to live again, I promise you."

Chapter 13

Reflection through Reading

It is not uncommon for people to reflect on life when they have much time alone, and from occasional conflict new horizons come into view, particularly in terms of quality relationships. I remembered discussing with Sophie a few days earlier about Lester and his infatuation with his girlfriend who was going out with someone else behind his back. He was obsessed with her but the relationship was going nowhere. I said that the tentative nature of relationships is shown where mothers of some children leave one abusive partner and enter another, and often very quickly:

"If having been bitten once, why are they not more cautious? Why rush into a further abusive relationship?" Sophie, as usual, came up with the simple answer.

"It's because people don't want to be alone." I could relate to that only too well.

I was reading a book at the time called *Stuart*, the story of a homeless man in Cambridge. One of the pertinent points the author articulated was how charities often have a misguided view that those who sleep on the streets in cardboard boxes have a totally miserable existence. What is it, the author asks, that draws these people to such a lifestyle when provisions in hostels and the like can be set up to give them support. One of the theories the book explores is that such homeless people experience comradeship and a sense of community from being 'on the streets'. I hadn't really thought of it before. What it means in practice is that removing the unsightly spectacle of homeless people from our city centres, and ridding the stigma of a beggar on the streets, involves organisations, charity institutions and well-meaning do-gooders finding them flats in which to live, but when such premises are found the destitute often become lonely, alienated and sometimes resort to suicide — as Stuart had done!

The next day I spent much of my time alone and so I finished reading my book, *Stuart*. I found the end quite disturbing when it featured quite graphic accounts of the main subject being abused by his brother, a babysitter and a teacher in a residential school. This was not the kind of reading I needed at this time. In conclusion, however, the author recorded a dialogue he had had with his subject on the cunning means by which ex-prisoners made claims for compensation — *that's interesting*, I thought!

After finishing Lionel Shriver's, *We Need to Talk about Kevin*, I shared with friends my thoughts on the novel. I found it a disturbing read, one that raised a number of issues for me, particularly over professional people choosing to have children late in life whilst still continuing their careers. The book leaves the reader enticingly drawn into interpreting non-explicit yet tantalising mysteries about a boy's secret life. It's cleverly structured as a series of letters that a mother writes to her murdered husband, in which she reflects on why it was that their son had elected one day to carry out nine murders in an American school.

Kevin was an enigma, a mystery, particularly for his mother who had viewed him as devious and cunning. At times the reader is left to interpret his callous behaviour as being caused by an 'insecure attachment' he had had with his mother, at other times he's presented as demonic and amoral. One feature that left me pondering was in regard to the nature of truth and the telling of lies. The author describes *the telling of lies as a well-honed practice whereby most of the details follow a well crafted account, accurate in detail and skilfully constructed, so as to lead the listener into a full acceptance of what has been claimed*:

'He had learned what all skilled liars register if they're ever to make a career of it: always appropriate as much of the truth as possible. A well-constructed lie is assembled largely from the alphabet blocks of fact, which will as easily make a pyramid as a platform'.

I suppose this had been what I had felt at the time— ambivalence. *What was the real truth? Is it a case of conscious deception or a question of differing perceptions?* I was troubled and in a state of indeterminate anxiety, knowing what would happen to me in the future, at what decision the CPS would arrive at and how my fate might be determined by the competence of a solicitor or barrister. There had been a part of me that would have relished a court case and the notoriety it would offer, bringing the facts into the open and exposing Alex for what he was. I even said to Daniel once,

"I wouldn't mind being a barrister having to defend myself and deconstructing Alex's accusation; that I'd love to pull holes in his story and explore what it was that had led him to go into the police station that day. But then going to court would finish my career, whatever the outcome—I couldn't function as a youth counsellor with any such publicity."

The August bank holiday weekend promised to be warm and sunny, and I had little to do of much importance. Normally I would have planned to attend a classic car rally or a stock car race on the Sunday, but given my situation I was left sitting, musing and generally feeling sorry for myself, yet again, wondering what I would do with my time, that un-targeted enemy of many bleak periods of my life. Thoughts came into my head from books I had read and from past calamities featured on the news. A young boy in Liverpool named Rhys Jones had been fatally shot whilst playing football with two friends. Apparently, it had been a case of 'mistaken identity' whereby a hooded youth on a bike took three shots and one bullet had fatally struck him. He just happened, as the police had reported, 'to be in the wrong place at the wrong time'.

What had troubled me about that pitiful affair was the apparent rise in gun culture that had been surprisingly at odds with reported crime figures of the period—there had been a 'reduction of offences involving guns' in the UK, according to statistics? Apart from being upset by the heartbroken appeal of his mother and father for more witnesses to come forward to reveal the identity of his killer, I had been concerned about an interview that a journalist had had with rival groups of young people on either side of the estate where Rhys had lived.

In both cases, when asked of the group whether any individuals would come forward with information that might lead to an arrest of Rhys' murderer, they all said, unequivocally, that they were not prepared to snitch on whoever may be involved, whatever the circumstances. Some boys covered their faces as the cameras panned around them, others turned away, but all were resolute in having no sympathy for the victim of an unjust killing through a pseudo-group loyalty and would not cooperate with the police.

Following news items featured senior police officers pleading with the public for more information but at the same time complaining about the lack of public willingness to provide information that would reveal the identity of Rhys' killer. *What sort of society is being shaped for tomorrow,* I mused, *where politicians appear to resort to the same tireless pledges of what they would do, or what should have been done, which have become little more than rehearsed rhetoric designed to win popular appeal. Politicians are so remote and out of touch with social conditions in some council estates.* This cold-bloodied dismissal of life had frightening echoes for me of *We Need to Talk About Kevin.*

A more academic book I had read during the period was entitled *Tomorrow's People*, a hypothetical study of the type of world in which we might live in the future with the escalation of science and technology. In that book, one question author Susan Greenfield poses is whether human beings will have the same amount of freewill, given the rise of terrorism in the world due to the shrinking borders of cultural identity. She makes the point that what terrorism feeds on is 'fear', which is cultivated within largely disenfranchised groups of young people who can be so easily indoctrinated to even lead them to surrender their own lives.

Daniel reminded me of a paper I had recently written on school violence that had drawn publicity in the local media. The paper commended a range of strategies for violently inclined young people to avert their aggression when managing personal conflict. Unfortunately, an unscrupulous journalist had selected one or two phrases from this paper and intimated that I was advocating the removal of high-risk children from their families, virtually from birth, where violence was endemic. He failed to realise that I was quoting from an American psychiatrist who had suggested that in families of deplorable parent modelling removal of children early was necessary and that incarceration of violent teenagers might be the only course of action to turn the tide of school killings. Our sensation-seeking editor had selected the writer's viewpoint and misattributed it to myself, which drew the attention of the local press and radio. Daniel was of the view that this may have triggered Alex to go to the police. I could not agree with his conjecture, but had acknowledged the plausibility of Alex construing that in the reporting I was making reference to his own family.

I read a book whilst on holiday in Tuscany, called *Galileo's Daughter*, a study that portrays the events leading to the trial of Galileo before the grand inquisition of the Holy Office. In one letter his daughter had written to him there were composed sentiments that I had felt were apt:

"The only thing for you to do now is to guard your good spirits, take care not to jeopardise your health with excessive worry, but direct your thoughts and hopes to God, who, like a tender, loving father, never abandons those who confide in Him and appeal to Him for help in time of need."

Galileo often used poetry to get his point across, but when illustrating the pre-eminence of one enlightened mind over the masses (i.e. of the Inquisition of the Holy Office) he speaks in single-minded resignation:

"In this the eighth week of my imprisonment, my mood tends to be more melancholy than depressive." I could relate to that at the time.

Love's Embrace by Brian Thorne is a personal autobiography of a person-centred therapist, and in that book the author described his earlier work at a therapeutic community in the 1960s. He spoke about his involvement with troubled adolescents in terms of 'honouring the uniqueness of those pupils who sought our support and validation'. In encountering unhappy and often emotionally damaged young men, he said, there was often a sense of abandonment as parents got on with their busy lives. Some had a hopeless desire to please parents by performing well to recompense them for the financial sacrifices for 'the best education'.

But the others would often be found staring out to sea on the promenade late at night having left their dormitories while their peers were asleep. During these days, he continued, it struck him how little was needed in some cases to rekindle hope and alleviate pain. Many of these boys had never simply been listened to — either at home or at school — and that for just 10 minutes of undivided attention they would find courage to battle on. That was my role in school.

This reading put me in touch with thoughts I had been having at the time, which centred on loneliness. Perhaps that's what we're trying to resist: the dread of isolation and being left alone. That's why adolescents bond with their peer group. That's why the teenager holds on to that first romance that is going nowhere. That's why some of us need a new partner when the last relationship has come to an end. And that's why the aged reach out to their offspring so as not to face ill health and their demise on their own — or as Paul Tillich expresses it 'the fear of non-being'!

Chapter 14

The Medical Report

On Saturday morning of the August bank holiday weekend, I was sitting in my conservatory with my good friend Rachel and my brother. The telephone rang and it was the investigating officer, DC Henderson, to tell me that he had received that morning the medical report from my consultant at the spinal injury unit and would in due course submit the file to the CPS, probably on the Tuesday, given that Monday was a bank holiday. He rearranged the date of my bail for the penultimate week in September, which he said might be brought forward if the CPS had returned a verdict. He also went on to say — and this was perhaps the first time that he had given me a glimmer of hope — that he may contact me before that date if the CPS 'threw the case out'. He was guarded in what he had said, obviously, but he clearly had inferred that this might be a possibility:

"Obviously, I can't say what will be the outcome."

"I quite understand, thank you very much."

For two days, I sat bored, waiting for a telephone call. I mused again on the two possibilities: either to be released and removed from my bail restrictions or to be charged and have to go to court. Once I had got over the first hurdle of knowing what decision the CPS would make, I could begin to fight back. I would have a voice again and could begin to sow the seeds of a new life. But until that time my fate and my prospects, my mental health and life fulfilment, lay solely in the hands of one other person. I rehearsed again, fruitlessly I know, the salient points for and against me being charged. Simply put, it had to be a case of Alex's word against mine.

As far as I knew, Alex had no corroborative evidence to support his claims, but there again neither had I to refute them. When I reviewed from an objective point of view any corroborative evidence to support my denial of what he had said, I have to say there was none—how can one prove a negative? From the officer's intimations, my defence solely relied upon the medical evidence in support of the fact that I was as disabled 16 years ago as I am today. If the report from the spinal unit were too technical then the decision would have to go to head office for a medically trained solicitor to evaluate its implications in terms of my physical disabilities.

What it all boiled down to was whether I had been sufficiently mobile 16 years ago to carry out what Alex had claimed I had done, as recorded on his statement.

Since the police (as I was told) were not required to ferret for extra information over and above what had been said in our respective statements, but rather to ascertain the authenticity of the conflicting 'stories' that Alex and I had alleged had taken place, it was difficult to see how the officer or CPS lawyer could arrive at an informed judgement without speaking with my consultant over the detailed nature of the accusations levelled against me, and since this would be prejudicial in a trial (should one occur), and indeed be conducting it without me being charged in the first instance, then I could not see that the report would tell them very much. It would mean by implication that the officer would have to talk personally with the consultant, or indeed to have had the consultant carry out an outpatient inspection of my motor power and compare it with the records of annual reviews.

Without such information, they would have been left with a 50-50 split decision on where the evidence had pointed. For this reason, as I had feared all along, and in spite of the officer inferring a positive outcome on the phone, I considered that I would still be charged on the bail date.

What stressed me particularly had been my limbo state of non-activity and my sense of powerlessness. If I'd have been a sheet metalworker or a vehicle technician working alongside adults, I could have carried on with my work regardless of being charged, since I would pose no particular risk to young people whilst being investigated, and even in the event that I were found guilty of being an offender my employment could have continued. But I was a foster carer and school counsellor who had daily engaged with young people in a confidential setting of adult and young person in a room with a closed door. For this reason, from the perspectives of the CPS, school and social services, a mistake to let a 'guilty person' go free and continue practising had to be avoided at all costs. Any notion of risk involved had to be eliminated. Whilst the accusation was over an activity that was alleged to have been carried out in my own home, not in my place of work, I still feared that since the Ian Huntley case there would be a tendency to err on the side of caution, to charge me so that a jury would have to decide the matter. Children may never again be placed in my foster care, but a conviction was required to stop me offering therapy for youngsters at school.

A conviction would have the effect of clearing all investigating officers, the CPS, social workers, foster care managers, school governors and Daniel, my headteacher, of any culpability should I have covertly abused young people through my office and position of trust. This was why I had been so negative over the past two days, and had remained so until such time that a call might come through. I can see why distraction is so effective in cognitive therapy for depression.

I went to bed that evening a little settled, but then awoke in the early hours filled with doubt again. No matter what friends and colleagues had said to encourage me, somehow I still felt deep down that I would be charged. *As each hour passed, I fantasied over the CPS lawyer and the investigating officer piecing together enough evidence to warrant charging me. I had thought the medical report would not provide the required information; it would not tell them clearly enough my abilities and restrictions to authenticate or refute his claim. It might give them all sorts of irrelevant details about my bladder and kidneys, such as the tests I have undergone annually as an outpatient, an operation I had received on the sphincter five years after my discharge, but the rest would be numerical figures of motor power and neurological functioning. It would not tell them whether I had the ability to shuffle about in a range of positions, since the consultant never tested this. It would also tell them, and confirm what I had said to the officer during my interview, that I had very little sense of feeling below my chest.*

So the CPS were left with the narratives as they had right from the beginning, which were Alex's version of events and my categorical denial of abusing him — Alex's word against mine. He had no corroborative evidence to support what he had said, and I suspected that the corroborative evidence the police were trying to examine would not tell them that much. It had appeared to be a 50-50 split. I was not able to authenticate my account and neither was Alex able to substantiate his.

For me the fantasy had run on in that *the longer the hours passed without a telephone call the more I had imagined the police looking for every possible shred of evidence by which to secure a conviction in court. Perhaps the CPS lawyer had felt it necessary to take the file into head office to have the medical report interpreted. Perhaps the report had been read and a final decision had been reached and that the reason why I hadn't been informed was because the investigating officer was not on duty.*

I believed that, contrary to continual reassurance of friends and acquaintances, *if the allegation had been so clearly unsupportable and the case weighed in my favour, then why hadn't the CPS rejected it on first reading without the need of the medical report for 'absolute confirmation'?* In my statement, I had not said 'it would be impossible to have performed physically what I was claimed to have done'; I said 'I doubt whether I could have done that'.

The charge was that I had touched Alex inappropriately on my bed, and that required that I should either have shuffled down the bed or that he would have had to have moved towards me. I was never able to shuffle down a bed, which was why the tailboard was significant I suppose. In other words, I had not, in that respect, denied as categorically that my handicapped condition would render me unable to do as Alex had claimed. This was because I had not been entirely sure what he had told the police. All I could do was to tell the truth and answer the specific questions that had been put to me, with the added qualification that Alex had never ever been on my bed, and that whilst staying over night he slept alone in the spare room.

My mind spiralled downwards into a negative abyss as the hours crawled forward and as the telephone remained mute. When would the call come? I knew the officer needed to make contact either that day or the next in order for me to sign a form to cancel the original bail date. Perhaps then I might know a little more, or perhaps then he would remain silent and leave me on tenterhooks over the outcome.

I had a small distraction the next morning when realising the MOT on the old Rover had expired. I arranged a test by ringing Bernard to ask for his support and this occurred on the Friday. That was a welcomed distraction. I still felt like someone about to take an exam, thinking: *the best way of approaching a nervous experience is to expect the worst but hope for the best.* I had been claiming to all my friends that I was pretty sure I would be charged. As I said to one friend:

"As I move closer to my bail date, it looks obvious I will be charged. After all, the CPS has now had my file for four complete days. Surely it wouldn't take that long to scan through the documents and arrive at a decision. If my case was so clear-cut, why should it depend upon the medical report anyway? Even if it had been sent to head office, should it take that long? No, I am sure that the closer we move towards that final bail date the more certain I am that I shall be charged, and my life as a counsellor and foster carer will be over." Naturally, in such a conversation, I was completely dispensing with comments that a former head and my current solicitor had made, that basically I may as well right off August in terms of proceedings moving forward at a reasonable pace, that matters may well move towards the end of September before resolution, and that at this time the three months speculated period would be complete.

Chapter 15

Pessimism to Resignation

My original bail date for the end of August had passed and I expected the officer to visit for a signature to extend the date of my revisit to the police station. *The sun had been shining that morning but I had not felt content with the world.* The new bail date for the end of September left me frustrated again through prolonged inactivity. *As each day past I moved inexorably towards the probability of being charged. Obviously, the fantasies took over objective reasoning since this is how we are made; at least this is the way I had become. The problem was that yesterday afternoon a range of facts coalesced in my mind, which gave a bleaker picture than that I thought my friends and colleagues had prepared me for — optimism for the sake of my sanity.*

What my ex-colleague Gordon had said the night before only made sense in my mind if Alex had accused me of assaulting him 'against his will'. Gordon asked me to reflect on the image that would be created as I came into the courtroom in a wheelchair and struggled to stand to my feet. He was inferring that the case would be by and largely won before I opened my mouth. But Alex had not claimed 'the assault' was 'against his will', far from it. This was my dilemma: how could I defend against what he had alleged — he had knowingly or otherwise covered all bases. It made me think that somebody smarter than Alex had put him up to it.

I recalled what my former student had said when advising that I should never underestimate the cunning of ex-offenders and what they learn from inmates in prison, even those who were formerly uneducated: they get to know the scams and wheezes, the devious ways of making money and how to use the system. *Perhaps, there is compensation in the minds of Alex and his accomplice, after all.*

What I thought would be difficult for a barrister to defend, and what must have been a puzzle in the minds of the investigating officers, was that Alex had not presented a narrative typical of an abused child in retrospect. He had not said that I had forced him to do something sexual, held him down by force and subjected him to an assault. He had claimed that he had enjoyed the sex and been 'aroused' by what had taken place, that he had intentions of coming back to my home frequently, and that he had still been fond of me. *Now how could I or anyone else defend against that? In light of that portrayal, my physical disability was largely irrelevant.*[8]

The only defence I appeared to have had was my reputation set against his and that he had still to prove what he claimed had taken place, and that meant, at the very least, appearing in court (something that I was unsure he would do in the final analysis). Further to this, his unusual, and certainly untypical, claims for having come forward will surely be interrogated. His sexual orientation and history would be brought out into the open along with mine, and I suspect in the event that he would be more injured in court than I would have been, not that I think he would have thought that far ahead.

I therefore considered myself as vulnerable, and possibly viewed as not being innocent in the eyes of the police at that stage, and for that reason I anticipated the CPS would press charges, if only to be on the safe side and not let a possible abuser of children slip the net. My statement to the police as to the reason why I stopped him coming to my home, whilst plausible on objective reasoning — *what was I saying, that is the truth, for God's sake!* — could equally play into the hands of Alex's defence and indeed support his charge. It could be argued logically that the reason why I stopped him coming was because indeed something 'had taken place' and that I was in fear that it might escalate beyond control, that I might later get discovered. The only defence remaining, from such a perspective, would be why Alex remained silent for as long as he did; and further how the alleged offense could be proved 'beyond all reasonable doubt'.

As I dwelt on this possibility, I imagined that the CPS had reviewed the case. *It was not as though the lawyer had seen the file for the first time — it had been available from bank holiday Tuesday to the Thursday morning of that week, over two full days. It would only have taken an hour or two at most to read through the documents and to arrive at a decision. The fact that the officer had not rung me must mean,* my fantasy continued, *that they had judged 'there was a case to answer' and that the only reason why there had been further delay was that the police were already building up a profile of how the case would go — a game plan so to speak.*

The officer had said that, although the bail date in September was set, it might be brought forward. *Now why would that be, I pondered? It must only be because they had already determined there was a case to answer and that there was no further need of extending the date. Why else would he wish to bring the bail date forward one or two weeks?*

Suicidal thoughts invaded my mind again, in spite of the pledge given to Patrick. I think this was because I simply could not stand being alone day in day out. I had to put up with this now for nearly three months; I simply could not imagine having to remain in this limbo state for a further nine to twelve months before a trial. I was not that much troubled about a trial; it was just the publicity. Having said that I later recalled a significant comment in Jodi Picoult's novel, *Salem Falls*:

'Conviction or acquittal could hang on whether the jury had a good breakfast that day.'

That's what depressed me, and the thought of not being able to cope becoming a Schedule 1 Offender. I had worked with troubled youngsters and had been stimulated by their spirit of living from the age of 17 to the current time, particularly when becoming a seriously disabled person. What promise could life hold out for me if I were found guilty?

I reviewed my will and made changes that needed to be made in the event of making an impulsive decision — ironically, I had included Alex as a beneficiary in my will. Reading a book like *Stuart* didn't exactly foster a positive outlook since he took his life by overdosing on heroin. But how on earth could I take my life in a way that would not be uncomfortable and painful? I have never taken drugs and wouldn't have the first idea where I could obtain them. My mind began to explore the possibilities.

Was it realistic to sit in my old classic car in the garage at the top of the garden and leave the engine running without bringing attention for sufficient time to be suffocated through exhaust fumes? Could I take enough paracetamol to take my life before being discovered and rushed into hospital? It's all very well to reason that this would be so damaging for Patrick, Chris, Lester, my brother, friends and colleagues, but they were not living the life I was having to live, and whilst they offered me support and occasional social engagement they could not be expected to be there 24/7. It was my disability that hindered me from having a fulfilled life.

As I have said, I'm not persuaded by the reasoning that suicide is a 'coward's way out'. I don't much care about whether or not the option of taking my life would suggest guilt. That's not the point. How is it possible that someone who had given his whole life of 50 years to helping and supporting many hundreds of young people end up a Schedule 1 Offender? That's the point. How fair is that? What sort of society rewards altruism with a conviction of assault through no reliable evidence other than a claimant's say so?

Patrick popped in and it was good to see him again. We spent the afternoon assembling a garden barbeque I had bought from a garden centre. I had the radio on and consequently could not hear the front doorbell ring. Whilst sitting in my conservatory with Patrick, I was surprised when the door opened and officer, DC Henderson, walked in. He had not met Patrick before and so had no idea who sat before him. Since seeing Patrick was not part of my bail restriction, I was not unduly alarmed. The officer handed me my new bail sheet. I asked Patrick to leave for a while, but as he arose from his seat the officer said,

"It's OK, you needn't leave.' I just wanted to deliver your bail form."

The revised bail date was set for the end of September, but he did say as he left that he would be in touch earlier if the decision had been reached before then.

Following that weekend, the staff would assemble to plan for the new academic year, and an opportunity for me to speak with them without the pupils being present would not be possible. No doubt, rumours would abound. I had until the Thursday, at least, before the main body of school pupils would return, and on Thursday morning I suspected that Chris would be disappointed not to have seen my car on the front car park indicating my return to school after an 'illness'.

I was invited to my friends, Frank and Hannah, for tea on the Friday night, and somehow felt a little more positive. I began to think differently about my case as I mulled over what I'd read and as thoughts came together with other comments that my former pupil had made about the mindset of those who had experience of prison life. *Look at my situation*, I reasoned with myself, from a different angle. *My spiral of negativity had taken a foothold from the fact that everything Alex had said was not only feasible, coherent, but also true — indeed, as though I would have to fight to maintain my innocence, innocence against the 'evidence' of a well-meaning citizen acting upon unselfish motives and interests?* What my student had said to me on the phone a few months back was that I should be very cautious about calling too many people for my defence without knowing where they're coming from. There's no shortage of unscrupulous folk prepared to make money, even at the expense of betraying past loyalty.

"You must remember," he said, "that you will only know Alex from the time you last met, and he's travelled a journey since then, just as you've done. In fact, you're virtually strangers now. You don't really know him at all. I can tell you," he further said, "These types of people, even if they're not particularly bright, learn all the scams to make money, particularly through compensation claims. He doesn't live the type of life that you do. He'll be drinking in back corners of pubs and talking to friends of his and fellow-crooks who'll know how it's done. You, my friend, have become a victim of what is becoming common. He's found an opportunity to screw you and make money at your expense. You've been stitched up my old friend. He's got no money, but he has got time on his side and many hours to kill . . . How do you think he spends his time; not going to work every day as you do. You earn a salary; he's got little by comparison. He's seen an opportunity of fixing you, and that's the reality. The positive thing, you must remember, is that the police will be aware of his past history — this type of thing is not new for the police, but it is for you."

A different picture was emerging. *Had the visit by Alex been fore-planned to work out how he might pull it off? Remember, he appeared 'from nowhere' — he was there all the time, perhaps even planning to break in till I turned up unexpectedly. Alternatively, was he waiting for me to arrive, knowing what time school finishes and my general routine? Was the purpose of his visit, unreasonably short as it had been, to look over my home? Why did he want to look at the classic cars in the garage if not to examine my disposable income? Was he not sussing me out? And why the six-month gap between this so-called 'social' visit and him making the allegation at the police station? Then, look at his reasons for coming forward.*

He claimed to be having an argument with his girlfriend for not being able to perform sexually, and his sexual dysfunction was due, as alleged, to something that had happened in the past between him and a teacher.

"Who's going to swallow that", reasoned my former student. I was considering all along that Alex was not very bright to work that out, but as he repeated "these people become educated in a certain form of criminality that looks ahead at all inconsistencies and contradictions of a story. They are skilled at this type of thing and well rehearsed in making alibis and inventing so-called 'facts'. And, perhaps, it may also indicate that he's not acting alone; somebody else is behind this! He would know that should he claim that sexual impropriety had taken place 'without his consent', as though forced into sex by an adult overpowering him, or that he had been simply confused at the time, it would not stand up in court."

"A former colleague had said to me that a jury just looking at my physical condition would realise his accusation was implausible, that it wouldn't stand up in court. Alex would look foolish," I added.

"He'd be pressed to account for why he kept returning, which, again, would not stand up in court, even if he claimed that he'd been aroused and had wanted sex. He'd have reasoned that a far better way would be to present a story that he had been complicit in the whole affair, that he had no objection to what took place, that he had wanted sex and that he had regretted that he couldn't engage sexually later on because he'd been 'damaged'. His plan is to have you done for abusive, though consenting, under aged sex. He'd still have been faced with the difficulty of whether there were sufficient grounds to claim compensation, if he willingly returned for sex, but at least it would have given him a start, and you're the adult, he's the kid. No, I think it's a plan cleverly devised with his mates, and you've been truly stitched up my friend."

After hearing that I may have been duped I felt disheartened. It wasn't due to guilt; it was just that I could see little way forward in providing a credible defence, that should a jury have a predisposition toward Alex's account over mine—simply because I was the adult and he a child of 13 at the time, and that such things have happened in the past—then the decision could go against me.

I had considered that the most profitable way for me to have continued, at least mentally, was to reason that I could do little else but start planning my defence in the event of the case going to court. I looked again at some of the claims that Alex had made that ran counter to my memory of what had actually happened:

What about, for example, his claim that he offered personal care in school. How could that have been credible, and indeed, acceptable ethically, in practice in a public institution like a large secondary school without concern being raised at the time by senior personnel? I said in my statement that personal care in school would have been highly irregular, and unnecessary, given that I have no such care needs during working hours.

I needed to secure a defence. *I should,* as my headteacher had advised, *attend to detail and set about to discount elements of his story that would leave in the mind of a jury doubt over the certainty of what Alex had claimed.* I decided to record these facts, and disputed facts, in a grid that would be useful for my solicitor to assemble a case for my defence.

What happened in the next few days, as pupils and teachers returned to school, was that I had felt again that empty solitude of non-engagement, of wondering how I should spend my time. It was Saturday morning and I attended to editing a manuscript for a new book.

During the next week, I felt disconnected from colleagues and from what had been till recently the centre of my working day existence. I only seemed to have had flashes of memory when meeting Patrick, or when looking at photos of kids at school, or hearing about systemic changes in the pastoral department. I was becoming resigned to accept whatever came along, or as a Taoist would say: *'let events roll on'.*

Friends and colleagues offered more regular support to keep me positive, and consistently believed there was a weak case to charge me, saying variously:

"How on earth can Alex or his brief prove that a historical indecent assault had taken place with no corroborative evidence, only his word?"

It seemed as though whatever impatient and negative feelings I had had, it was likely that my file would be given high priority. There was the issue of making sense of the medical report, then, as Allen had said, the police were now required to be highly professional with their investigation, and finally holiday leave for practitioners inevitably holds things up.

When I told Daniel of the delay, he said that he had received a telephone call to say that the PPOT meeting scheduled for the first week in September had been postponed a further month, and that this would mean I would not be returning to school till the first week in October at the earliest, whatever decision the police had arrived at. *I was going to have to sit this out, and prepare myself for a much longer haul than I had anticipated.*

I began to drift into a mindset of: '*Charge me, if you bloody well want to. Prove what has been alleged against me if that's what you think is necessary.* My neighbour called with a cup of tea in his hand and I shared with him recent news. On knowing of my work with wayward kids over the years, he had always remained convinced that I shouldn't have to defend myself, and he also said that the police were not likely to rush this through, given that we were still in the holiday season. He further said that I should remember how the police would view people like Alex. I reminded him of the way he had presented himself: *as a model citizen wishing to safeguard the innocence of other young people who might fall prey to my indiscretion.* He said in reply,

"No, they're crooks. He's a crook! No one is going to believe that a person like him had high-minded principles. He's only looking after himself, that's the way he'll be viewed and no one will take him seriously. He appears to have a range of questionable motives, and people will see through him."

A conversation with Jason on the phone a little later that afternoon seemed to support what my neighbour had said. Jason also asked me to imagine what the implications of being charged would be. He began to tell me of a headteacher who had been accused of physical assault and was away from her work for a whole year. When the case was heard she was acquitted and went back to work, but only for one term. He said that it was important for her to return to establish her dignity, even though she was weeks away from retirement. There would have been little time, and, it might be argued, little point in going back. I had to admit that I had not thought of this before and so I began to review earlier thoughts I'd had which were that *if it took too long I simply could not imagine returning to school and having to cope with the inevitable rumours that would have circulated and taken root through the passage of time.*

I had now thought that Jason may be right and that I might have to consider that in the worst case scenario, so long as I was acquitted, then I would have to return to work, albeit for a short period given that my job was bound to change anyway.[9] This kind of positive thinking had been setting my mind at peace and I felt more able to put up with the torment of inactivity and to put my life on hold for a further few weeks, after all what else could I do?

I reported to Jason what my solicitor had said that whatever the outcome there would be a written statement on my CRB recording in lurid details Alex's allegation against me, even if I were acquitted in court and even if I were never charged in the first place. There is no context, no right of reply, no defence—no opportunity to counter-argue his claim, just stark prose of damning assertion.

Chapter 16

Call of Reprieve

On Tuesday evening in early September, at approximately 6 p.m., I received a telephone call. It had been a fairly uneventful day and I was sitting in my conservatory, as was my custom for the past three months. My friend Jason had paid me a visit in the early afternoon on his new superbike, and my brother was staying for a week's holiday. The telephone call was from the investigating officer, DC Henderson, it was fairly formal and to the point, lasting little more than three minutes or so. I was in a fairly 'matter of fact' mood and could hardly register what he had said as I thanked him before putting the phone down. From optimism to pessimism, from high expectation and anticipation to resignation and acquiescence, I hardly knew how to respond.

"Hello Richard, it's Chester here, DC Henderson. I rang to let you know that the CPS has now examined the file. The police are to take no further action . . . The matter is now closed as far as we're concerned." I took in breath and paid greater attention to the actual words spoken. "I actually knew yesterday, and would normally have spoken with Alex first, but since I haven't been able to contact him I thought I'd let you know the outcome . . . You won't have need to speak with Alex in the next few days, will you?" *What sort of question was that?*

"No, I don't think so!"

"Good. I'll write to Alex and you'll have a letter in due course." I didn't know how to feel. He continued. "Now, regarding your work situation, the police have no say in that but I do have to attend a final meeting with social services in early October. I shall be contacting the Chair to try and bring that forward; there's no point in dragging this on any longer."

His words had not sunk in initially and I offered no sentiment of surprise; I was stunned as though in a trance. The answer I had long awaited left me stupefied and unresponsive. There were so many questions I wanted to ask him, but none were voiced. My response was un-emotive as though his call had no significance, as though I had been accepted in a talent audition in which I didn't really want to take part. Hiding my relief, courtesy took over.

"Chester, I'd like to say how impressed I've been with your professionalism in the way you've conducted this investigation. It's been a harrowing experience for me, I don't mind admitting, but in the end it is in my interest as much as anyone else's that the investigation has been thorough. I'd also like to say I'm grateful you've kept a lid on things . . . I've had no direct evidence of rumours spreading from your enquiries, and, I suppose, although it's been long for me the final decision hasn't been that long in the order of things." His voice slowed and became less-official, more off the record.

"Thank you. Actually we had a case not too dissimilar to yours and it bothered me that it took five full weeks before the CPS arrived at a decision. I made a complaint about the time the defendant had to wait for an answer. I think it was because the same CPS lawyer was dealing with your case and she'd remembered that. I'd caught her on Monday when she had a spare block of time and we sat down and went through the file together . . . Now I do have your book that I'll have to return."

"I'm not worried about that, Chester. Please accept it as a gift, and let's hope it can help your dad with what he's going through. Perhaps now that this is over you'd like to pop in one day when you're passing for a cup of tea?" He never responded, positively or negatively; I suppose it wouldn't be fitting.

For thirty minutes or so, I had no idea how to react; I still felt shell-shocked and numb. It hadn't fully sunk in what the officer had said. I should have jumped up and down in exhilaration, immediately reached for the phone and rung everyone—tell the world the news—but I just sat there, stultified and not sure how to feel. As thoughts of release began to pervade it began to dawn on me that I had now got my life back. There was indeed going to be a brighter tomorrow after all, the sun would shine again, and I felt like a prisoner receiving pardon from death row, like a paralysed man sprinting away, like I'd been given a million pounds.

Shortly after the call, my brother returned and was quite animated over how his day had gone. He led the conversation for 30 minutes in energised fashion, telling me of his achievements that day. I waited for him to finish his monologue and just let my news slip in, almost as an afterthought.

"The police called today, just before you came in. They said the case was going no further." I shared the full account of what he had said over a cup of tea. I shared the news with my homecarer when she called and then telephoned my neighbour across the road. He was so jubilant he left his meal and came round with a glass of lager to pass on his sense of relief and jubilation. As we all sat in the conservatory, I stressed how low I had felt up to the call — which he had registered along with my homecarers — and I pointed to the garage at the top of the garden (visible from the conservatory window) and said that that was where I had planned to take my life. I stressed how serious I had been when contemplating ending it all by leaving the engine running, expecting that no one would find me gone for a time, till at least the following morning.

I was not sure how much my closest friends were aware of how close I had come to taking my life. I think it was probably only Patrick and thoughts of little Chris, and a hopeful reuniting, or at least the thought of what it might do to them should I take my life, that prevented me from rushing into impulsive action. Who knows? Why I brought this up at this point when I should have been ecstatic I don't really know.

After it had finally dawned on me what the officer had said, the whole evening was then spent telephoning friends and colleagues. First I contacted various headteachers to pass on the news. They were thrilled on my behalf and insisted that I should have a drink of wine on them. Daniel said that he would be consulting the legal department the next morning to see what procedures he would have to follow in order to reinstate me. The penny had finally dropped and I could hardly believe such conversations were taking place. The nightmare was truly over. The first and greatest of all my hurdles had been cleared and the rest seemed trivial by comparison. I rang my friends, Frank and Roger, and they were over the moon to such an extent that I could hear their company cheering in the background as though a party were taking place. I rang Patrick and his mother and they were equally delighted, although Patrick and his mum were becoming increasingly anxious about their own situation. I rang one of my homecare tuck-in girls and she immediately popped round after work for a nightcap and chocolate bar. Though there were many telephone calls I needed to make, there were not enough hours in the evening, since all calls lasted well over an hour. I brought my Scottish friends up to date before deciding to close the day and retire to bed.

Curiously, it was a very restless sleep, but for very different reasons. I was excited like a little boy having freedom in a candy store, and during my restless sleep my thoughts kept returning to being back at school. I always knew that Patrick would be loyal, that our friendship was well sealed and that a bond had formed that would never be lost irrespective of the outcome of his or my case. But with little Chris, I could not be so sure. Should I have been charged, or worse still found guilty, I would probably never see him again.

There was not a day that went by without me thinking about him. I couldn't fathom why it was that thoughts of him continually invaded my consciousness. It may have been something to do with his hardship and his spirit of fortitude to overcome his lack of adequate parenting. Putting to one side the fact that his mother and father had rejected him and his siblings and turned to heroin abuse, I think it was also the fact that we had shared good times together in a very short period of time. We had common interests in classic cars and I was benefiting from him becoming my best car mechanic ever. Knowing him to be unhappy, and in care, I was quite prepared to offer him a home and become his foster parent. What had brought him regularly to mind was not only looking at the old cars in the garage, but something on the floor by the door. As I walked through my garage and on into the conservatory I would glance at his old trainers sitting motionless and unoccupied.

In the morning I was a little insensitive to my dedicated homecarer. I sat on the bed and announced to her that the police had made contact and said that in view of the seriousness of the allegation made against me they regretted to have to inform me that they had no option but to charge me and that the case would be going to court.

"Well, never mind; you thought that might happen, didn't you."

"No, I'm only kidding. The police have told me that I have no case to answer. I'm free of all bail restrictions." She was duped and looked momentarily cross.

"Oh," she yelled, "Why did you do that to me . . . ? I'll get you back for that. I'm so thrilled." She threw her arms around me and gave me a hug. This was the beginning of a new day and a new life, and perhaps I may soon begin to answer that question posed for me a few months back by Sophie, which was to speculate on what God was telling me through this experience.

"He took your body when you broke your back. What do you think he's teaching you through this?" This question might take a long time to answer. Before going out the next day, I drafted changes that I felt were necessary to my job description to better safeguard myself so that Daniel was prepared for the final PPOT meeting.

Chapter 17

Beginning a New Life

The next few days were taken up with extensive telephone calls, telling all my friends of the outcome and decision of the CPS. Calls to Daniel, my headteacher, were the most pressing, since he had begun to plan for the closing PPOT meeting. He informed me that the earliest possible date would be during the first week of October. A telephone call to my teacher association representative informed me that I might have to face a Disciplinary Meeting arranged by the head. 'This is merely jumping through hoops. For some heads it's a formality, but many teachers experience it as being quite informal. It's just the procedure'.

Disciplinary Meetings normally take place after the CPS have thrown out a case and have elected to go no further through the lack of evidence. The principal concern is to make sure that 'all children are kept safe', and officials are aware that just because the police have decided to take no further action this does not mean that the welfare of children in school is thereby safeguarded; it only means that a claim is unsubstantiated and that it would not be in the public interest to hear the case in a criminal court without more evidence to secure a conviction.

During this week I spoke regularly by phone to my headteacher. He had been busy negotiating with the LEA over the extent of his authority and formal responsibility to reinstate me before the PPOT meeting had been convened.

This was to prove a battle of Titans. I was aware that both officiating chief officers (one employed by social services, the other by the LEA) were red-hot over procedures being followed by the letter, but it seemed in my case as though there was a principle of justice at stake by not reinstating me before the closing PPOT multi-agency meeting. Since my case was a historical allegation over something that did not happen in school but (allegedly) occurred in my home, and indeed in light of the fact that my professional conduct in my place of employment had never been in question, it would appear that the procedures did not fully cover my particular situation.

Human Resources informed the head that it was his responsibility through the Chair of Governors to reinstate me, and that there was no need for this to take place subsequent to the PPOT meeting, as long as a Reinstatement/Disciplinary Meeting was officially convened with minutes taken. Daniel consulted a further expert in legal matters regarding education procedure, and he confirmed that so long as he had held a formal meeting to reinstate me then he could see no reason why it should not be done as soon as could be arranged.

Daniel contacted the LEA official of the PPOT core group, whose principle role was to serve as the leading officer over disputes of this kind that involve employees in regard to child protection allegations, and he put it to her that he was intending to reinstate me in light of the fact that two officials were unable to reschedule the meeting in less than three weeks time. Her reply took him by surprise. She said, in effect, that in that case there was little point in having the closing PPOT meeting. Daniel replied that she could choose not to meet again if that was her wish, but that he was quite prepared to clear his diary and attend the PPOT meeting at any time, or on the scheduled date if the meeting still went ahead as planned.

Further conversations my headteacher had had with social services managers were becoming fraught and contentious. He informed one leading official that he did not see any reason why he should even discipline me:

"What has he done?" The officer replied that she didn't know, nor could she know until the closing PPOT meeting. His conversation with her went something along these lines:

"Can I ask whose decision it is to reinstate Mr Lewis? "

"Well, it's yours. "

"That's fine; then I'll reinstate him as soon as I can arrange it, unless we can agree to meet this week . . . I'm quite prepared to clear my diary of all my other commitments to fit this in. "

"That will not be possible." She and her colleague, I believe, had holidays booked. She further said, "I cannot see how you can reinstate Richard Lewis without hearing what recommendations the meeting makes over the accusation!" There were power games going on here!

"Let's put it this way. I understand that social workers have interviewed Patrick who had been bailed to Mr Lewis' home and have come up with no concerns. The case has been closed. And I'm led to believe that at least one young person formerly fostered by Mr Lewis has been interviewed. So, unless you're privy to information that I should know about, that should inform my decision, then after taking advice I will reinstate Mr Lewis. "

"I don't see how you can do this. You may be required to carry out your own investigation. "

"Investigation, investigation of what? What is the evidence against Mr Lewis?" This conversation was becoming circular and was going nowhere.

"You could approach the police and ask to see the file."

"Ask for the file! The investigation is the job of the police. I'm a headteacher running a large secondary school. How can I carry out an investigation — that's why the police are part of the multi-strategy meeting. And besides I have full confidence in Mr Lewis' integrity, otherwise I wouldn't be prepared to reinstate him."

"These are the procedures . . ."

"You seem to want to run a kangaroo court?"

"No, they are the procedures . . . You don't believe the boy then?"

"You mean 'I don't believe the *man*. No I don't, as a matter of fact. Do you?"

"I don't know without seeing the evidence."

Throughout the entire process, I was aware that the particular regional social services managers, and particularly the principal officer who had a reputation (even amongst her own team) of being close-minded and self-opinionated, were going to be a much more formidable stumbling block than the police or my employers would ever have been. The attitude displayed by one principal officer in multi-strategy meetings and justified in the 'name of' protecting the welfare of children always troubled me when I served on a child protection advisory team. A significant number of headteachers in the area felt the same. It was as though other professionals had not that concern as their fundamental principle when working with children and young people, as though she was the last bastion of child welfare for the city against a tide of foster carers and teachers who set out to harm children.

In preparation for the closing PPOT meeting, Daniel and I agreed the following changes to my working/social involvement with pupils of the school:

> ➢ Never to permit a young person ever to sleep overnight at my home, even if their parents were in agreement
> ➢ Never to take a pupil on holiday with me again, without the full knowledge and sanctioning of social services

I pledged that I would no longer put myself at risk. Daniel agreed that since my counselling role in school was not in question, but that it was only my personal involvement with youngsters in my home that was the central issue and focus of the allegation, this was where changes would need to have been made. Changes to fostering were to be made by teenage fostering personnel at a later date, since there was need to suspend me from fostering as from counselling young people following the accusation.

My solicitor informed me that the investigating officer would compose the actual record of accusation made against me on future CRB documents, but that such wording could be appealed against and altered if it was factually inaccurate or if I didn't think the phrasing reflected what Alex had insinuated.

She suggested that I might get a better outcome, in terms of what may be worded, if I wrote a letter to the chief constable commending DC Henderson's work if I had felt he deserved recognition. A record was entered in my journal and further telephone calls were made before the day closed.

On Friday morning I took a trip out to see Gordon for light lunch, and it was a sunny morning. I particularly enjoy this journey because it offers an opportunity for reflection over the half-hour trip along the motorway. I began to think of something my teacher association representative said regarding the forthcoming PPOT meeting. He was annoyed that it was to take five full weeks before this meeting could be convened to close the matter, and I began to get angry myself over why it was so necessary for this meeting to take place at all let alone be drawn out. He informed me that it was a change in procedures and that it was one of a series of hoops that I would have to jump through, and I agreed I would have to dance to the fiddler's tune.

"You'd think that they could find someone to stand in if they're all on holiday." I had said to him that it concerned me that I might be treated differently after the allegation, even if it had been refuted.

"I want to now go about my business as though an allegation had never been made in the first place."

"I know what you're saying, but in my experience that never happens."

"I don't think that will be my experience." *I was innocent till proven guilty and in light of the police enquiry turning up with nothing I remain an innocent person.* "On both of my letters of suspension, from school and from the fostering service, it is expressly stated that the action of suspension is 'without prejudice'. I want to feel that this happens in practice as well as in principle. I will have enough to cope with dealing with the possible rumours that may have circulated to have to worry about what social services stipulate as a condition of my employment. If I am told that I should not permit young people to be in my car then that will be OK so long as it is a rule applied to all members of staff. If I am instructed that no pupils are to attend my home then again that's OK so long as that is outlined to all other personnel of the school. In other words, I want to be treated as though no allegation had ever been made against me at all." In reply, he said that what I had felt should be true, but that in his experience it's rarely the case.

"Many accused teachers tell me that they are treated differently, particularly by their headteachers after such an enquiry. Most feel that they are stigmatised after child protection procedures have closed. Headteachers want to be rid of some of them if they're a liability."

"I suppose that's because of undue publicity, and for having to manage too many confrontations between pupils, parents and teachers", I replied. He said that that might indeed be the case, but that it's still a common experience for teachers. In conclusion, I said that I was confident that that wouldn't be the case for me.

I was now about half way on my trip when I began to reflect on my anger. A few teachers have asked me the inevitable question of 'what will happen to Alex now it's all over?' This has been a regular annoyance and remains an issue for teachers. As I sit typing my journal, I have a newspaper cutting in front of me making the same point in wake of the rising tide of false allegations against teachers.[10]

So when asked whether I was angry with Alex, my answer had always been no, paradoxically. He was just an opportunist looking for a chance to make money, perhaps, or certainly to get some attention from an otherwise uneventful life, or, according to his testimony, if it is to be believed, to save face over his lack of sexual virility. Whatever the case, I had not been as angry with Alex as I had with the system. I began to wonder what it was that was prompting this new and growing feeling of resentment, and I think it had something to do with a system in which I had little confidence.

> ➢ I was angry that it took three months to arrive at a decision, a prediction I had made from having to manage teacher's cases of child protection accusations in the past.
>
> ➢ I was angry at being left to flounder by three major departments, with not the slightest support from professional bodies that were preoccupied with a wish to 'cover their backs'. No department offered official or therapeutic support; it was left to individuals like headteachers who were privy to my case. If I were any more volatile, I may not have coped and may indeed have taken my life—having so many friends to turn to, I had a means of preserving my mental health.
>
> ➢ I was angry about having to answer so many damn questions, yet again, about my sexual preference. I know such questioning is imperative, but it is tiresome

to have to provide the same details before a questioner whom I had imagined would be sceptical about my claim to be straight and not having deviant sexual interest in young boys.

> I was angry because I was not trusted, or believed, in some quarters, as indeed I would later find out. I anticipated being judged by the belief that 'there's no smoke without fire', rather than by evidence from the testimonies of hundreds of young people.

> I was angry that I would be prejudged because of not being an 'ordinary guy', not having a conventional lifestyle; that I should be made to feel guilty because I had given my life to help deter young people from delinquency rather than get married and have a family.

> I was very angry that having been cleared by the police and the CPS, this was only the beginning of being under suspicion. I was not able to return to my post after the CPS decision. What was so frustrating was that if the officer had notified the Chairperson of the PPOT meeting immediately the CPS had arrived at their decision, then the meeting could have continued on the scheduled date, two days following, and myself to have returned to work the next day.

The officer wanted to inform Alex before me of the decision, but couldn't make contact, and further had assumed that a meeting would have been convened within the week, but this had not been possible due to planned holidays. *Why could not officials have been deputised to stand in*, I raged? I suspect the answer was that the meeting of closure would not have been considered 'high priority'. If a major incident had occurred, let's say involving a headteacher in systematic child abuse, a PPOT meeting would have been convened 'the very next day, let alone the following week', whoever may have been on holiday.

This is what I found so irksome. There's no doubt my personal welfare, and a sense of justice, would not be considered very important. I had no illusions about that. But in not being prepared to meet earlier, or at least find a suitable person to deputise, inadvertently denies the pupils access to their counsellor and thereby *the wellbeing of other pupils* is being put on one side owing to the lack of flexibility within the system. Both the police officer and Daniel were quite prepared to alter their diary commitments to bring the meeting forward; it was only two principal officers of the strategy group who refused to have deputies stand in.

> ➢ I was angry about the kind of messages my experience was giving to voluntary helpers of vulnerable young people, and also, as my cousin had said, about the kind of society that is being shaped inadvertently through inflexible, top-heavy child protection procedures and health and safety protocols.[11]

I rang the manager of the teenage fostering service to inform him that the police had cleared me and he appeared relieved with the outcome, but further concerns were raised for me when he spoke of the current stance of the department with regard to future fostering plans with professionals.

He told me that the managers of organised abuse and allegations against staff were always glad when the school holidays arrived, because their workload tended to ease. He said that there are four times as many allegations against teachers as there are against foster carers, but adding that there were five other foster carers currently under investigation from allegations of children of their current or past placement. I said to him that if this continues there is going to be a considerable shortfall of people putting themselves forward for fostering.

"We're going to have an increase of children desperately in need of love, care and support with fewer people coming forward through fear of allegations made against them. We have to get this right."

He agreed. I then went on to speak with him about my future role as a foster carer and he told me of the decision of the principal manager to ban teachers and social workers fostering young people with whom they have had a previous professional engagement. Asking why this was the case, he said that although it seemed ideal in one respect, the problem is that if a child is being abused by a social worker, or a teacher, then it is difficult for that child or young person to speak out. They would feel their complaint would not be taken seriously and that the department would show bias if a worker or teacher was abusing them. I acknowledged this in reply, but then said:

"But surely this is solving one problem from a negative point of view. My most successful placements were two lads who were pupils from my school and, by contrast, those less successful were previously unknown referrals of the department. I bonded better with the former group. Why should such critical a decision like carer-child matching be determined by the lowest denominator of whether an allegation will be believed?"

"I know what you mean."

"I would be prepared to foster Chris now this is all over, but your boss seems to be saying that wouldn't be possible. Surely any decision to foster a child should be made on the basis of what can be of mutual benefit—how could I enhance the development of this young person etc. Surely, we shouldn't be making decisions wholly on the basis of allegations being heard. How disheartening," I concluded.

Chapter 18

Back to School

I felt that my status had altered and I was beginning to get my life back. The sun was shining on the Monday morning; in fact the sun shone virtually every day since I'd heard of my reprieve, not only metaphorically but also literally each day was brighter.

I set about to examine what may need to be done in order to enter school and cope with the rumours that I had suspected would have circulated. I speculated on how a few clerical staff might interpret Patrick leaving my home. I had no doubt — in light of what he and his sister had picked up — that there must have been suspicion and that people would have talked.

I felt this was confirmed when Patrick's mum told me that her daughter had become perplexed by questions put to her about her brother being removed from my home, and this required careful management.

Inevitably, I would have to offset well-meant messages of concern over my 'illness' and it was not easy anticipating what I might say if people had known the truth. I planned to speak with some staff I had trusted to explore the extent of rumours in circulation after the Reinstatement Meeting. My neighbour's wife, a fellow teacher, had said that in her experience such a rumour would be all round the school by now. Still, I would have to cross that bridge when coming to it, take it a step at a time, but then my presence in the building would to some extent allay further rumours.

On Wednesday morning in mid September, I attended a formal meeting of reinstatement. This entailed a convivial conversation with my head over a cup of tea as we got down to business and followed the necessary procedure. The following day I entered school by driving along my regular route. It seemed surreal. I could hardly believe what was taking place. A few pressing questions remained unanswerable:

- *How I would be received?*
- *How would I address genuine sentiments of being glad to see me back, of being happy to know that I was 'better', when in reality they may have known the true reason for my absence?*
- *Who would I have in-depth conversations with about the whole affair?*
- *Would I have the opportunity to speak with Christopher, and, perhaps, Patrick's sister? What should I say?*

These matters of course were impossible to plan for — fantasy rules as much as reality in such cases. I'd have to let events roll on and take their course.

Approaching the front drive, I steadily moved towards my parking lot. Three girls met me and offered to fetch my wheelchair. Opening my door, I was met by the school nurse on her way in. I had telephoned her the previous day to say that I would be coming into school the following day, and she said that she was sorry not to have returned my call because she only took the message at the end of the day. I said that that was OK and that perhaps we might have a little chat later. As the girls brought my wheelchair to the vehicle, Chris approached from the rear of my car. My heart fluttered as I looked at him and said

"I missed you Chris."

"Me too," he replied. "Would you like me to get your things out the car and open up?"

"Yea, thanks. We'll have a little chat later on today." Chris opened the rear door and took my carrier bags and keys and proceeded to open up the counselling room. I could hardly believe what was taking place, one of my pupil friends once again helping, being reunited with the one person I had missed so much over the last three months and to have the opportunity of sitting with him and exchanging each other's news — *and perhaps leap the last hurdle.*

The member of staff I engaged with first was an attendance worker I had trusted, and I briefly shared with her the reason why I was absent from school. She was genuinely surprised, and was most insistent that she had not been aware of the reason for my absence, and that in her opinion most teachers accepted the story as purported, that I had been off school because I was unwell. *I had to reconsider whether I was wrong in thinking that gossip had passed around the building and that everyone would be too polite to bring up the matter in conversation. I would have to play this by ear, I decided. Certainly, fantasy had taken over reality.*

I arranged to speak with Chris during period two, when he had technology. I was somewhat apprehensive as to how much detail to share, but was certainly looking forward to engaging with him. He made us both a drink and sat down in his usual seat. This was our first conversation in three months, and for me it was a difficult occasion, largely because I was unsure whether I should say anything at all about what had happened, whether it might be better to leave him with the agreed explanation of my absence from school.

My most pressing concern however was that I knew, as I suspected he knew, that there was nothing stopping me from contacting him on his mobile phone. *Three months is a long time, and surely I thought that he would think that I should have been well enough to give him a call; that I couldn't have been that ill not to have spoken to him on the phone? How do you explain to a young lad of 13, especially one in the care system, that his counsellor had been accused of assaulting a young boy 16 years ago when he was only Christopher's age?* Both parents rejected Chris and I didn't want him to feel that I had done the same, but how could I tell him that the choice of making no contact was not left to me?

I explained to him that my absence was not due to illness entirely, but to something that happened that I found highly stressful, but that I could not share it with him at this time. In a few weeks time, maybe, I would meet with him and Patrick and tell him everything that had happened. I shared with him that he was not to take my failure to contact him as a personal decision, since I had been so instructed by others not to make contact with any pupil of the school. I finally said that I had thought about him often. Above all, I wanted him to trust me.

In retrospect, I was not sure I did the right thing. He looked a little mystified; perhaps I'd said too much, spoken in riddles that left him even more perplexed? Perhaps it might have been better — as Patrick had advised — to have left him with the explanation of my illness preventing me from coming to school. One of my peer counsellors came into my room at that point, and to some extent her arrival brought to an end our first meeting. Chris lightened up and became more cheery in one sense, but in another looked a little frustrated that our time together had been interrupted. I explained to him that I had felt it would be best if he did not help me after school for the next few days, yet he also anticipated this by saying the same, until, as he said, "I've spoken to my auntie".

I had other conversations through the day with pupils I had known well. I spoke also with my teacher-friend, Clive, and had a fuller conversation with a deputy headteacher I had known for many years. I told him the truth, but wondered whether he had known already. He told me of something I was not aware of before, which was that he had suffered a similar experience in that a pupil had made an allegation of physical assault against him and another teacher at an outward bound centre. He explained that he was very angry about the comments that had been placed on his CRB form. He was also apologetic about not popping in to see me over the holiday, since he lived close by and was aware I had been absent for so long.

Towards the end of the day, I spoke with my line manager, and he similarly was supportive, being aware of the anxiety I was under. He spoke derisively of social service officers having little common sense and being preoccupied with 'covering their backs'. It seems that there was common agreement that education and social services were poles apart in terms of working together.

I spoke to Chris the next day at the close of the week for 20 minutes and said to him that my plans were to get back to normal, and that I particularly would like to spend time with him and Patrick as before my period of absence. I asked him again what his aspirations for the future were, and he replied as before.

"I still want to be a car mechanic." I pledged to support him to reach his goal whatever that turned out to be, but I reminded him that his auntie was not always happy about those occasions when he had returned late after helping me, that we have to respect her wishes to get you home on time. He resented being under tight control. He grumbled about having to be in bed for 9.00, and his sister at 16 by 9.30, and that this had been the worst six weeks holiday of his life. He also resented her making false claims for welfare benefit. He didn't like living with his auntie, but I was also aware that he disliked being told off by those in authority, a sign that he was still non-conforming. I said to him that in many respects accepting discipline brings more progress in learning at school, that being under tight control was not so bad, even though this was something he resented.

I said to him in closing that I would like him to help me again after school, and for him to visit weekends when the time was right, and to carry out jobs on the car, so long as this is what he had wanted, and as long as his auntie and social worker granted him permission.

My feelings for little Chris had not diminished, and I felt just as fond of him as before. He was the reason I kept my sanity. He prevented me from taking my life and gave me hope to continue the fight. It became clear that it would have been inappropriate to tell him anything else about the reason for my absence — he was too young to handle that or even comprehend it. I did not want him to become over-burdened with something that was too difficult to handle; I just wanted him to know that my commitment to him was still strong.

I was aware of the promises I had made to get him into motocross, but that it might take some time before we could get to that point. As he left he said that he would not be in school on Monday because he had a dental appointment, which he was not looking forward to. I replied that I would give him a call to see how things had gone.

On the Friday evening at the end of the week, I took Daniel and his wife out to dinner at a local restaurant and we had a splendid meal together. I expressed my gratitude for the support he had given me over this difficult period. It was a sunny weekend, and my heart skipped in-tune with a gentle autumn breeze. I had arranged a barbecue that weekend and it became the best of the year. Each of the previous occasions with friends and family were held when I had the sword Damocles over my head, and as such were not for me relaxed occasions, but this one was the zenith. Not only had I really enjoyed it and felt free at last, Jen and Paul travelled from Scotland to join us.

There was a local Steam Festival on the Sunday, which I would love to have attended, but only having just got back into routine there had been no time to organise support. I had considered going alone, but then thought it would be of little value since my weekend helper was coming to pack away things after our barbecue. On the whole I couldn't believe what had happened throughout that week.

- I had been to school for a formal Reinstatement Meeting, and spent two full days in my former post
- I had seen nearly all the pupils I had regularly worked with
- I had spoken to chief personnel who were informed of what had happened
- I had communicated with Chris.

Over the week Patrick attended court and considered whether it was worth returning to my home. It was his 16th birthday on the Tuesday and I got him a card and gift, but I hadn't seen very much of him through the week at school. On the Tuesday I called Christopher's auntie because he had not been in school for the second day running, and although I knew he had attended the dentist on the Monday I was concerned he may have had a hard time with his treatment—he was certainly very apprehensive about going. She explained that he could not receive his treatment that day because the dentist wanted parental consent and, since his social worker had not been available to get the necessary signature from his mother, it turned out to be a wasted journey. In the event he attended the following day and had four back teeth removed. She went on to explain that Chris had expressed a wish to help me again after school. I said to her that if Chris wanted to help me, I was happy to receive his support, so long as full approval had been obtained from the social worker — this was done.

On putting the phone down I became jubilant. I could hardly believe what she had said. It seems that my last hurdle had been leapt over prematurely. I was the happiest person alive. *Was it possible that after three months of hell I could now go back to school as though nothing had happened, returning to my previous state?*

I was back at school and it was as though I'd never been away. Yes there was the meeting to come in October, but I had little fear of what that would entail that could affect my current situation. It seemed to me that it would be just a case of 'ticking boxes' to show that the professionals had covered 'every eventuality' and had once again avoided all 'culpability'.

Chris had become my assistant after school and my heart began to dance as each day became once again fulfilling. Had he resigned to live with his auntie, until 16 at least? I had no idea. I was content to let time pass, and at this point I was enjoying life to the full.

Over the next week, I counselled two clients that particularly gave me a sense of importance in school. One was a boy of 16 who had become pessimistic and had dreaded daily life. He had become overwhelmed with a sense of morbidity. He suffered from epilepsy and was on strict medication, but one Saturday night he had a seizure that scared him. His mother told him all the bizarre visions he said he had seen, though he was unaware of what he had told her during the seizure. This left him mystified and in dread, feeling that he was losing his mind. As a means of preventing a repeat seizure, he took twice the prescribed medication, nearly overdosed and was sure he was dying, refusing to come to school. He recovered under a programme of cognitive therapy.

The second client was a girl of mixed race who had been thrown out of her home by her mother. She had never known her father, who was black, but her mother now resented her, largely due to attitude and the colour of her skin, which she had no reservations in stating very publicly, even amongst her friends. Her mother was in a new relationship and had another (white) child, and she could no longer tolerate her 14-year-old daughter. She pushed her out onto the street, but when her daughter found another home with her friend's mother she resented this and refused to give her permission, stating that social services should pick up the case. I identified with her sense of loneliness and gave her regular companionship through counselling support.

I was clearly back at work again and running on all cylinders, and with Chris supporting me at the end of each day I had felt as though my nightmare had come to a close. All I had to wait for was the closing PPOT meeting to finalise the matter. The following Monday, however, there was a pleasant surprise. When pulling up at Christopher's home, he remained in the car and looked at me with doleful eyes and said:

"I'm going to ask my auntie if she'll let me start coming to yours."

"That would be great, Chris, I'll look forward to that — perhaps I could get some fish and chips." I turned to face him as he left the car and he said:

"See you tomorrow."

As each day passed, it looked more likely that I would be able to return to my former quality of life, as though nothing could further tighten my chains of paralysis. I woke up on Saturday morning to a good English breakfast after having had my second complete week back at school. This had been such an exhilarating week that I could hardly believe that switches in mood could take place so rapidly. At one point some nine weeks ago I had contemplated suicide, but at this point I was full of vigour and looking forward to the weekend.

The high point was the occasion when Chris said he wanted to ask his auntie if he could begin coming over again. And when that time came it felt right to share his company. In one brief evening, he had replaced three light bulbs in my porch, had picked ripe damsons left hanging from a tree, and had lifted the bonnet of the Rover and discovered the reason why the temperature gauge had failed to work. Naturally, we had our fish and chip supper and it was lovely to see him cleaning his plate again, leaving the delicacy of the fish till last, as was his practice. Just before leaving to take him home I said:

"It's great to have you back Chris."

"It's great to be back, I really missed you."

In spite of what my teacher representative had forecasted, it appeared as though things were back to normal as though the allegation had never been made. I was out of the gloomy long tunnel of despair. The head and I met a couple of times to finalise his presentations to the closing PPOT multi-agency meeting. We had agreed the form of words with which my pledge was to be made, whereby I was vowing that I would not allow youngsters to ever sleep again at my home except through the auspices of social services, and that I would never again take on holiday alone with me a pupil of the school who was under the age of 16. Those were the only commitments I felt were applicable to the allegation, and the head was in full agreement.

Other discussions centred on the possibility that members of the meeting might wish to make the recommendation that no pupils should ever be allowed to visit my home at all. We explored the implications of this requirement and felt on balance that it was impossible to secure this condition in order to avoid any possibility of future allegations being made against me. I shared with him a discussion I had had with Jason, a mutual friend, over tea, when we had looked at possible occasions where pupils might have cause to be in the home of a teacher.

- What about if a teacher offered private tuition to a pupil of the school?
- What about in cases of fostering a young person who may have friends of the school where you work?
- Should I be required in that instance not to allow a fostered child—with the auspices and full agreement of social services—to have friends visit him at our home simply because of the fear of future allegations?

No, much as I loathed that period of imprisonment, I could not allow myself to be re-shackled with impossible requirements simply to satisfy professionals who had appeared to have not the slightest interest in the needs of a particular young person, only in the interests of 'covering backs' to avoid all risks. We had both realised that impractical pledges were pointless, and I felt Daniel was prepared to counter requirements of absolute and unworkable guarantees.

I was grateful for his sensitive management over future arrangements, because he was all too aware that this was what had given my life meaning, and that, even in the final years towards retirement, enriching the lives of youngsters in school, living in impoverished conditions, was my vocation. All that had now remained was to await that meeting, and in closing our conversations we both had wondered whether or not it might turn out to be a damp squib.

Chapter 19

The PPOT Meeting

On a Monday morning early in October the closing PPOT multi-agency strategy meeting took place. It had been a tiring day on this the first day of my third week back at school, and after a departmental meeting the head caught me at the end of the day to share the conclusions reached at the PPOT meeting. He looked tired and a little troubled as we made our way to the private setting of the counselling room. The news he gave made my heart sink. Although I had always suspected that social service officers would be my greatest opposition, I wasn't quite prepared for the venom of their final bite.

Daniel said, quite bluntly, that this had been a controversial meeting, that he felt alone in supporting my position and that he was personally facing criticism for reinstating me before the final PPOT meeting. He related how the police had reported on the decision of the CPS and the recommendation that no further action was to be taken, and the rationale of their decision. He also explained to me how he said his piece, indicating, I suppose, the pledges I had made in moving forward, but I don't think even he was prepared for what followed.

Almost as a rehearsed mantra, the Chairperson, a principal social services officer for allegations against teachers, foster carers and other professionals, and the team manager of the local area office managing the case, voiced serious concern about closing the case and were vitriolic about the fact that an obvious paedophile had still been left in a position of trust among young people in a secondary school. Time and again, it would appear, the Chair kept saying that she had heard 'bells ringing' every time details of my life story had been related.

'There is something alarming', she expounded, 'about a teacher having no regular partner inviting boys to his home . . . There's something really wrong with what has been going on here.'

They recommended that Daniel should reconsider his decision to reinstate me and to carry out his own criminal investigation — even by requiring the police to release information stored in their file for him to view.

As a final recommendation, the Chair instructed the manager of the teenage fostering service to carry out his own investigation before contemplating reinstatement. The Chair closed the meeting by saying that she would report back to her senior manager outlining her concerns of the outcome of closure of this case. At one point, the area officer asked what would now happen (i.e., after the CPS closure and with my reinstatement at school) in light of there being 'no evidence' of an assault having taken place, and yet with the perceptions of at least two principal officers (who had no idea of the sort of person I was) believing I was a paedophile from 'typical patterns' of 'grooming behaviour'. The Chair (with great regret, I was sure) concluded that there was no procedural basis for not bringing the enquiry to an end.

I think it was at this point that Daniel realised why I had been so apprehensive the minute the allegation had been made against me; I think even he was not as attuned as myself in knowing how the system would work and how it would be prejudiced against a professional with a lifestyle like mine if an allegation were to occur. Even he had not anticipated the avalanche of insult and abuse against my person that would take place.

Clearly, there was no point in further discussions. Their minds were made up long before the meeting had started, and the team of social workers remained resolute in the 'incontrovertible facts' that I, 'as a paedophile', had slipped the net and was free to operate in my former post, unopposed and without restriction. *There was no question in their minds of the certainty of this deduction, because for them the signs were clearly evident. The Chairperson had conducted the meeting partially and had dominated discussion through her sentiment of the 'bells that kept ringing in her ears' in spite of no supportive 'evidence' for such a view. It was for them typical 'grooming behaviour': a single person with no partner in life, regular behaviour of inviting pupils to his home, and using his position of power to prey on the young and vulnerable.*

As the head related what had taken place, I realised of course, as did he, that I would be unable to fight back against such outlandish defamation of character, since he had shared with me information that was only for those present, and I, above all else, had no choice but to accept the boundaries of information sharing—I could in no way act upon what he shared. Needless to say, I was outraged!

As I drove home I became increasingly angry by the minute. It was as though all that pent up emotion and hurt that had simmered over the last three months had now boiled over. I told Lester the outcome of this meeting and he was equally disturbed and voiced his personal views of my character:

"If it hadn't have been for you I wouldn't be where I am today [a qualified car mechanic]. You're not a paedophile, in no way."

I hadn't slept much that night because I could see that the golden moment of reuniting with Chris might have to be reviewed. Although I could not envisage the PPOT managers having direct links with Chris's social worker, or team managers, there were principles at stake and, as has always been my manner in life, I didn't want to engage with him secretly — there was approaching the time when I would have to disclose to his social worker that a historical allegation had been made against me but that I had now been cleared. Whilst I had permission to engage with Chris at my home from his social worker, this was not with the foreknowledge that a historical allegation had been made. A moral dilemma had left me with a choice of balancing justice with principle, openness with innocence.

Communications had been regularly taking place with Chris' social worker and team manager long before recent events, and although according to British law a subject is innocent till proven guilty there is still the issue of integrity. The key question was 'should I inform Chris' key workers of the allegation in light of the CPS decision and the PPOT proceedings having now closed and my status as an approved foster parent still under 'suspension', albeit 'without prejudice'?

A telephone conversation to the fostering agency manager had confirmed that details of an unfounded accusation and closed enquiry would not be kept on a database held by social services. Only those personnel involved in the PPOT meetings are privy to such information. *I am a free and innocent man and there is no law or principle preventing me from engaging with Christopher or anyone else; should officials reason otherwise, they would have to provide very good reason, but then Chris was a 'Looked after Child'.*

As things turned out, I had planned to speak with Daniel first thing in the morning and to have shared with him how angry I had become the more I reflected upon statements made at the PPOT meeting:

"How dare they castigate me and berate my personality in such a way, saying that I fitted the profile of a paedophile? None of them know me personally; they're going on perceptions and prejudices. Why was it that the manager of the fostering agency *[who should be fully conversant with my lifestyle — the material was regularly covered during supervision and annual reviews with my link worker]* chose to be silent? Why didn't he speak up for me? All my fostering link workers knew I had invited pupils of the school to come over to my house; they saw kids like Lester as an asset to the placement, and yet in light of my involvement with kids at school they were still happy to place four lads in my fostering care. Why was that?" I was fuming. "Why wouldn't the manager speak-up on my behalf instead of leaving it all to you? Did the Chair dominate them all? Are they all bullied by her?"

"It seems as though they are. I was angry the more I thought about the implications of what they'd said. It was a travesty. They don't care about you; they're all 'covering their backs'", replied the head.

"But what grounds have they to accuse me of being a paedophile?" I further asked.

"I don't know."

"They say I fit the profile of a paedophile because I've had lads at home working on classic cars to keep them out of trouble. I do get involved with kids on the edge of trouble with the police, but does this make me a paedophile? There are other details about my life that don't fit the paedophile profile. Paedophiles cannot help themselves and cannot stop defiling kids; in spite of the risks of being found out they can't resist their drive to keep abusing youngsters. They almost relish the risk involved as much as the sexual gratification. They act covertly, secretly grooming isolated children to lure them away. They pick on the most vulnerable as targets. Alex is the 'only person' to have made an allegation, and yet there have been literally hundreds of kids I've worked with — even at my home — who hold me in high regard and who would rally round to my defence if this had ever gone to court. I'm very public, not secret. My life has been widely published." I sighed heavily as Daniel allowed me to further rant.

"They castigate me and know nothing about me; they've not investigated me themselves. This boils down to them not being happy I've been reinstated without their sanction and approval; that's what this is all about. I'm back at work before they had a chance of influencing your decision — that's what's got to them, being denied power.

In over 30 years of working with kids, and having supported so many through counselling, has it not occurred to them that before Alex's allegation there's never been 'one single sniff of impropriety' levelled against me. Hasn't this been thought untypical of paedophilia? Paedophiles abuse kids repeatedly, secretly and covertly; I'm very public; everybody knows some kids come to my home. I write my life story in books, for goodness sake! And I don't 'select' the vulnerable and easily influenced as though they're prey. I take on the toughest characters of the school, those like Patrick, those who certainly would never allow anyone to tamper with them sexually should I be that way inclined. Have they not considered the contra-indicators of paedophile behaviour? She appears to have high-jacked the meeting with prejudicial steering?" I rested for Daniel to interject, since I was beginning to repeat myself.

I was angry, and so was he. He then said to me:

"Well, at least it's all over; the matter's now closed. You have some consolation there." He had attempted to lift my spirit and be optimistic, and I welcomed that.

"I don't really think so, Dan," I said, "It's not as simple as that. The Chair still has influence to counter any future possibilities of me fostering kids again, and it's going to be very interesting to see how they handle my reinstatement as a foster carer, given that they can't find evidence to prevent it from happening. Naturally, as social workers, they're all singing from the same hymn sheet; they're all part of the same team, so they'll try their damnedest to find reasons not to have me back into the fold. I'll follow my normal routines with youngsters I've been involved with in the past, honouring my pledge and sticking to the rules."

I elected to behave in ignorance of what Daniel had reported, as though I had no idea of what had been said. Yet I would protest, and protest publicly, within all professional quarters, if prejudice influenced that final decision.

"It's going to be very interesting to see how the next few weeks pan out in terms of my fostering position and reinstatement." In closing, I asked him about the team manager of the local area office of social services, since I had had much involvement with him over the years in planning child protection protocols for secondary schools in the area. His reply was disheartening:

"Well, in what he was saying at the meeting, I certainly wouldn't trust him!"

"Oh dear!"

Chapter 20

Reinstatement with the Teenage Fostering Team

Nearly two months had passed, and I felt I should contact the manager of the teenage fostering team to enquire about at what stage his investigation prior to reinstatement as an approved foster carer had reached. As I had said to Daniel, my headteacher, it would be interesting to see what reasoning they would put forward if they chose not to reinstate me, given that the police had dropped the case through lack of evidence, and that he, my employer, had taken me on again to be fully engaged with young people. If I am judged to be safe in that context, why should I not be safe in all others?

On a Wednesday morning in November I met the manager and link worker of the city's fostering team to review my status as a foster parent of 'looked after children' — a meeting I had asked for since no correspondence had taken place and I had wanted closure. This meeting proved to be largely inconsequential but it was clear nevertheless that there were still political factors overriding the decision of the manager to reinstate me to my former position.

He allowed me to open the meeting and to suggest an agenda. I had felt a need to engage in an honest exchange of viewpoints rather than become drawn to defensive sword fencing. I made this plain in my opening introduction where I stated that I had felt that we both might profit through speaking 'frankly' over the allegation, and subsequent investigation, in view of the seriousness of his decision to place children again in my care. I said that at this point I was not wholly sure I wanted to foster again and that I had no preconceived plans at this juncture. His reply made it clear that he did not want to take part in any other meeting than a strictly formal one, and, as I glanced across the table at my link worker diligently taking notes, it became instantly clear that politics were again overriding:

"Is that what you think this meeting is Richard, an informal one?"

"I'm not sure how you want to view this meeting, but there's clearly unfinished business with the fostering department which needs closure now that two months have elapsed since the final PPOT multi-strategy meeting."

In some ways our ensuing conversation became mutually guarded, in others we spoke openly when defences were down. I shared with him the stress I had been under throughout the entire process and the considerable disappointment I had experienced when all professional agencies connected with social services had effectively withdrawn emotional and therapeutic support. He became defensive at this point:

"I hope you don't think that we would not have been willing to offer you support Richard." I chose not to give him the answer I think he wanted, but thought to myself: *if the cap fits* . . . . In point of fact, as I had shared with Daniel, I did feel that support from the fostering service was notably, and surprisingly, lacking if not completely absent. An insinuation voiced at the closing PPOT meeting that my lifestyle resembled that of a typical paedophile could have been, and should have been, challenged and refuted by the fostering manager as indefensibly pejorative and slanderous. After all, his department through my link worker were fully conversant with my lifestyle through six-monthly reviews and had still elected to place young people under my care till demand had dropped.

The manager then took the initiative and prescribed two options. He suggested:

"In light of what you've been through, you could tender your resignation as a foster carer with the department. You could call it a day following the harrowing experience of being subjected to a child protection investigation. You could consider not putting yourself through the possibility of going through that trauma again, build a Chinese wall in effect, and then that would be the end of the matter. Alternatively, you might say to me that I still want to be considered eligible for fostering." I interrupted immediately and said that the second option would be my position, though I clearly knew by his emphasis what choice he wanted me to make.

"You see," I continued, "for a child protection enquiry to be fair and just and to have legitimacy it must allow for the possibility that a suspect may *actually be innocent* and as a result permit the suspected person to feel completely vindicated and absolved of shame and suspicion. I may be viewed as a predatory charlatan who has infiltrated amongst young people and hoodwinked three successive headteachers, countless colleagues, parents and youngsters, friends and acquaintances for over 30 years, by subtly grooming techniques in manipulating unsuspecting youngsters to be lured into locations for sexual favours from a powerful position of trust. Alternatively, I may be viewed as a totally innocent person who has suffered the necessary formalities of an investigation arising from an unsubstantiated allegation. The system, as far as social services are concerned, has made me feel like the former, whilst the investigation, as far as the police, my friends and education colleagues are concerned, has resulted in making me feel like the latter."

He began to question whether I had fully considered the implications of fostering again following a child abuse accusation. I explained to him that I had not been clear about that, but that I certainly wanted to re-establish my reputation, since I had felt there was a slight against my name and an air of suspicion amongst senior social services managers and the teenage fostering team.

He revealed his hand further with questions I had not anticipated, which I felt were politically dubious.

"May I ask your age, Richard?"

"I am 60. Why do you ask?" *My date of birth would be on file.*

"I can top you by three years," he joked, before going on to say that he didn't want to come over as being ageist but that it was not conventional for the department to foster children to parents over the age of 60. I was surprised by this claim—knowing of a few foster parents of 60 plus years having younger children than have been customarily placed with me (one 'looked after pupil' at school at the time had a carer of 68). He added further that the types of young people now coming forward are casualties of Somalia with severe traumatic needs. They're children in need of therapeutic support and it wouldn't be appropriate to place such children with you — *does he not know that as a professional youth counsellor I am more qualified than most to meet such need?* He then said that for these reasons the department looks for foster parents out of the city and from outside agencies even though it's more expensive.

"And as I said to you in a previous telephone conversation, the senior manager does not favour placing young people with professionals like teachers and social workers whose day-to-day contact involves them engaging with the same children [*recalling this comment irritated me again. The fact that placements today have to begin from the basis of how to minimise any possibility of allegations being made rather than meeting the social and emotional needs of a given youngster!*]. Fostering agencies are more generously equipped than we are . . . Our key workers have to manage as many as 20 cases, whilst many agency link workers only have to manage 10. They have better access to psychological support whereas we have long waiting lists, for up to six months or more."

I felt he was trying — quite successfully — to put me off any intention of further fostering children through his department, indicating he had misgivings about reinstatement even at a time of high demand and limited resources. I stressed that there was a point of principle at stake in my case, and that this was my chief wish for us to meet, if only to remove the stigma of being still held under suspicion. He asked for further clarification and I went on to explain.

"I have grave concerns about some of the sentiments that I believe may have been voiced in the closing PPOT multi-strategy meeting." He informed me that I had a right of appeal if I did not feel that the matter had been dealt with fairly and professionally. I added that I could not make any such appeal because I had not been privy to the minutes. The only thing I shared with him — being careful not to let on that I had a gist of what was said — was that my headteacher had left that closing meeting angry because he felt I had been judged not upon the weight of evidence against me, but upon my lifestyle as one as befits a particular profile of a 'typical paedophile' — whatever that might mean!

"In terms of process", he concluded, "as you're probably aware I have to carry out an investigation, but I cannot begin that until I have received the minutes of the three PPOT multi-strategy meetings, and I have requested those in three e-mails to the Chair but have as yet not received a reply. I expect I'll have to draw a line on this at some point soon and carry out my own investigation without having the minutes before me."

He pledged that he would further contact the Chair with a view to getting hold of the minutes and to speed up the process. "Should I have any concerns, I will share them with you so that you'll have a clear view of my findings." I thanked him for his time and left.

As I drove away from the meeting, I felt despondent due to the realisation that there's no way I would be approved again as a foster carer with the city's team, even for respite care. I reported this back to Daniel who had felt that his excuse for not carrying out his investigation till this time 'because he hadn't received the minutes' was invalid:

"That's bollocks", he said. "He was there at all but one of those meetings, certainly where the most salient details were given out."

Two months later, I received the minutes of that meeting from my link worker. After a further two months, I attended a second meeting with the manager and link worker to complete the investigation the fostering service was instructed to carry out at the closing PPOT meeting. I took with me my dear friend Jason, who served to listen, to interpret and to make notes. The meeting lasted one and a half hours and was fairly congenial and thorough. The manager first informed me that he had now received the minutes of the PPOT meetings, and this had given him the information he required to conduct his investigation. I shared with Jason prior to the meeting that I was not sure what to have expected from this meeting — whether he would complete his enquiry exclusively from the minutes or, as an alternative, interview me from his own notes and recollections. As it turned out, the former was the case, and it seemed as though the minutes became the basis upon which to compose a range of questions for the investigation.

The major part of the interview centred upon my role as a school counsellor, in which he was interested to know of the procedures and practices of pupils being referred to me. He had taken a particular interest in my engagement with social workers over the period of time and had appeared suitably impressed that I could drop names of principal personnel I had worked with who were considered today to be authorities in the field of child and adolescent mental health.

I outlined that my engagement with young people at home was more in the nature of offered support for a disabled person, rather than clients in therapy socialising with their therapist, and that such youngsters would not be described or understood as 'vulnerable' or 'impressionable' young people but those having high risks of delinquency and challenging behaviour, that my engagement with them was aimed at diverting them from street crime. I was not sure whether he was wholly satisfied with my motives for engaging young people outside of school, but I did have to stress that many of these youngsters were not principally past clients, which I had felt had been his presupposition.

When it came to the details of the allegation, he seemed well informed, and it appeared as though the minutes must have been a verbatim record of what the police officer had shared in the first PPOT meeting. At the close of this meeting the manager asked me whether I had any questions and I said I had none, but Jason asked about the process and where matters might move from this point onward. He informed us that he would have to write a full report within two full weeks, and that he would pass it to his line manager, who would then refer the matter to the panel for a decision. We exchanged courtesies and then left.

I telephoned my headteacher that evening to tell him how the meeting had gone and he was intrigued as to why the minutes had not been sent to him — in spite of two requests — when the fostering manager had clearly received his copy, indicating that they were indeed available. According to another headteacher, this may be more a question of 'cock-up than conspiracy'.

On reflection at home the following day, I wondered whether I had made it sufficiently clear that social workers of respective foster children, and principally my two link workers, were fully aware of my involvement with youngsters of the school in my home. I felt at one point that it might have been in my interest to write a short letter to stress this significant point not stressed by me at the meeting. I was feeling unsure as to whether I would be judged negatively on the basis of having youngsters of the school visit my home; that such behaviour might not wholly conform to current 'safe caring practice'.

I did not want to be penalised due to the fact that both social workers and link workers were fully cognisant of my customary social links with school pupils at home, and that, in full awareness, the department had still felt confident to place young people under my care. Jason's view was that I should hold back and save such arguments if I was not to be reinstated, that such detail would form the basis of an appeal.

Daniel caught up with me after Easter and said that the Director had called his judgement into question. He had received a letter prior to the holiday asking him to justify why he had reinstated me before the closing PPOT meeting — obviously, a complaint from the Chair of the PPOT meeting had filtered through the corridors of power.

It would not be appropriate to cover the detail of the meeting convened by the Director involving him, a senior manager of Children's Services, and Daniel with his representative, for this is another story. Needless to say, my headteacher appeared to have handled this meeting professionally, with integrity and with impunity, resulting in a resolution that had exposed the shallow sentimentality and hypocrisy of those managers in a 'position of power'. It had also become evident to me why it was that Daniel had found the closing PPOT meeting such a harrowing experience. It was not exclusively because I had been in the dock, but rather that he had been on trial for reinstating me 'against procedural guidelines' out of a sense of justice.

Jason, my friend and fellow foster carer, drew my attention to something I had overlooked in a pamphlet he had passed to me. This document described the procedures with regard to foster care and accusations of child abuse after police proceedings came to a close. It said that a fostering agency might carry out a re-assessment of a foster parent after formal police enquiries had completed with a verdict of 'no case to answer'. It then struck me that this was the procedural get-out clause they had been seeking — that they would use the situation to assess me as being unsuitable to further foster children.

This directive could authorise a decision that might deny me becoming further involved with young Chris, to cease all further contact with him within a pretext of fostering. Whilst at this stage my eligibility to foster was still left open, once the decision had been made it would seem that Christopher's social worker (who was replaced by a worker I had worked with in the past and in whom I had confided over the details of the allegation) would be compelled to share that with his team manager. And although his team manager knew me fairly well, and was pleased to have leaned on me to support Chris through a crisis, this was not in an awareness of an allegation having been made or that my status as a carer was left undecided. Certainly, the managers of the PPOT meeting would not have been aware of my engagement with Chris. When the consequence of this realisation began to dawn on me, I became a little down again and wondered, *what's the point of it all?*

A telephone call to my friend Gordon had settled my mind somewhat when he told me that all I could really do was to sit it out, that I didn't have to do anything at all but just wait. At the first PPOT meeting, the Chair had suggested that Daniel might consider pursuing a course of offering me incentives for early retirement, but he had dismissed this and had risked for my benefit curtailing procedures by reinstating me before the closing PPOT meeting in order to promote justice—his head as much as mine was on the block. And if the fostering management considered that I wasn't suitable as a foster carer, then that would be their decision and I would no longer be able to meet regularly with Chris. In other words, in both cases, I had no control over the outcome and I had to accept it. If the case went to appeal then perhaps I had a further year or so to prolong decisions, but then who knows what the future would hold in a year's time.

In mid May, nearly three months after the fostering investigation meeting, I wrote a letter prompting the manager for a decision and asked him at what stage his investigation had reached. He called me back two weeks later to say that he had completed his report two weeks after seeing me, as he had promised, and had passed it on to his line manager. He said that he had spoken to her again after receiving my letter and that she had said she would have to discuss the matter with the Head of Services. In closing, he told me his recommendation and said:

"There were never 'alarm bells ringing' for me, Richard". *How curious, I thought, that he used the same metaphor as the Chair had done but to opposite effect. Perhaps I was wrong in thinking he was 'bullied' by her, perhaps he's a wily old fox who was mute in the meeting because he knew her all too well, that he was playing a cute political game by going along with her directing but forming his own judgement and thinking more objectively?*

I corresponded with his manager in June enquiring about the stage of the investigation. I wrote in forthright style and said that should I not have had a satisfactory reply within two weeks I would take up the matter with the appropriate ombudsman. I quoted a paragraph from the same pamphlet Jason had given me which indicated that her department had not acted procedurally and was operating way outside the timescale of completing an investigation in a maximum of 27 days.[12]

She replied promptly to acknowledge she had received my letter in her office four day's later with the words: 'I am looking into the matters you raised and will respond in due course.' I received a formal letter two weeks later indicating that the manager of Children's Services could find no reason not to reinstate me as an approved foster carer for the city, and that from the specified date I was fully reinstated.

When I showed Daniel the letter, we could hardly believe its content. He in turn wrote to the Director passing on the news of my reinstatement, asking, enticingly, whether the managers of the fostering team could equally anticipate justifying their decision to reinstate, particularly since they are thereby endorsing young people to 'stay in the home of Mr Lewis overnight' not merely to 'meet with him publicly in a school setting'. Needless to say, there was never a reply. This meant, in theory at least, I had been fully vindicated and cleared of all suspicion to continue in my post of school counsellor and as an approved foster carer for the council.

Chapter 21

The Sequel for Patrick and Christopher

Patrick

Although during this difficult period Patrick and I suffered a different dilemma due to very different alleged offences, in a sense we had travelled a similar road together. I thought it necessary to spend an hour with him looking over the documents and witness statements before his trial. His situation looked bleak in view of the witnesses that were to speak against him. When I read carefully through the paperwork, it seemed as though a certain amount of license and embroidery had been going on during composition. Some of the recorded details of prosecution—police and ambulance logs etc.—didn't fit together, but it would take more than just a cursory glance at the statements to see the inconsistencies of recorded events in the paperwork; it would take a perceptive counsel to bring them out and build a defence.

On Wednesday the third week in October, the trial of Patrick took place at the city crown court. I was not able to attend on the first day owing to school commitments but would have found it a fruitless journey had I have done so, since there were complications over the jury being sworn in. Nevertheless, I attended the following two days. Patrick looked increasingly troubled on how the case had been going, believing that the jury appeared to believe the accounts of the plaintiff and his witness rather than those of his own family who had also witnessed the scene.

Following the case from a neutral perspective, I felt the barrister for the prosecution was much more astute and slick than Patrick's defending brief. The case for the prosecution rested upon a claim that Patrick had stabbed a man of 18 years who suffered from cerebral palsy. The family felt that because of the plaintiff's disability the jury would side against Patrick whatever evidence was presented. The prosecution called upon one witness and friend of the plaintiff, a girl of 14, who had claimed in her first statement (taken only an hour after the incident) that she had not seen a knife which the plaintiff had claimed had been pushed into his back, but then in a later statement (taken four weeks afterwards) she said that she had not only seen a knife being held against the plaintiff's throat with threatening gestures but could describe it in great detail.

This detail of 'evidence' was said by Patrick and his sisters to be invented and, since the alleged stabbing took place in what was claimed as a second encounter, I have to say, in view of the narrowness of the timeframe, and the distance between locations, that it could not have taken place in the manner alleged.

Patrick's defence was that he had come to the rescue of a known yet harmless alcoholic in the area who had received bruises to his face from pieces of tarmac that a group of young people had hurled at him in a nearby park. Patrick had challenged the main instigator and as a result received a head butt to his face before a fight ensued, a fight in which he came out the better. After the brawl, the aggressor ran away but his older (disabled) brother approached Patrick to reprimand him for 'fighting' his brother. Patrick admits to pushing him to the ground, but adamantly claimed there was no weapon involved — only five minutes had passed after I had dropped him off at his home that particular evening, which counter-argued premeditation.

Secondly, although Patrick had a volatile nature, as a person who would fight, he was known commonly as a person not to carry knives. Any injuries to the plaintiff's back, from Patrick's perspective, could only have occurred (possibly and feasibly) from broken glass or some other sharp implement as he had fallen in the long grass of the parkland pathway.

After the fight, Patrick and his sisters claimed they had returned home and had remained there being attended to by his mother only five minutes before the police arrived to arrest him and search for a knife.

As I sat during the trial, it occurred to me that there had been four salient points that the defending barrister failed to pick up on. One was the fact that only one event could have taken place within the 10 minute period (from when I had dropped Patrick off at his home to a logged call by the ambulance drivers to the police). The second was a claim that Patrick 'had been viewed' in different locations — a second over a mile away from the parkland. The third piece of vital evidence, unchallenged, was the nature of serious contradictions of the alleged use of a knife. And the fourth piece of evidence left floating in the air was the witness's claim that she had pulled 'some material from the plaintiff's coat' from a hole in his back, which resulted in 'blood gushing out'. Since the police had secured the clothing as an exhibit, I was surprised the counsel didn't draw on this material as evidence in Patrick's defence.

In the event, and largely through considerable steering of the jury by the judge, I felt, Patrick was found guilty of Count 2 Section 18 serious wounding by use of a weapon, but found not guilty of Count 1 that the wounding was 'intended to cause grievous bodily harm'. Patrick became forlorn after the verdict and the judge warned him that he could expect to lose his liberty in three weeks time after the pre-sentence reports had been presented.

Patrick was understandably upset afterwards and spoke for a short while with his barrister who had advised him that in the pre-sentence report he might consider writing a letter of apology to the victim, but only if he had felt he was able to do this without jeopardising his integrity.[13] On leaving the courtroom, I was being pushed in my wheelchair by Patrick's dad and in the lift on the way down to ground floor we had a private conversation. I asked him:

"Off the record, man to man, just the two of us, do you think Patrick did stab him?"

"I really don't think he did. He would have told me if he'd have done."

"Neither do I think he did. Still we have to face the reality of Patrick's situation and seek the best possible outcome in minimising his sentence." We both agreed.

Patrick was approaching his last week of freedom before having to return to court for sentencing, and a discussion with the Youth Offender Probation Officer raised some interesting queries when compiling his report. He said he would recommend that Patrick should receive a Community Service Order, but that he also said that he would be doubtful whether the judge would go along with this. I reiterated for him what the judge had said at the trial, how he had said that Patrick could expect to lose his liberty, which, as the Probation Officer reasoned, appeared to suggest that Patrick would go down for one to three years. But then, in light of that being in his mind, why did he not remand Patrick in custody instead of releasing him of all bail conditions?

It has been sad for me to reflect that I had been cleared whereas Patrick was found guilty; that I was never charged and yet Patrick had been convicted; that I had returned to work but that he had had to be tagged for three months under condition that he would not be out of home after 7.30 p.m. I spoke to Daniel the following day and he made a comment which I thought was fitting, that when you watch television programmes you get the impression that all barristers in court trials are sharp and skilled at discriminating truth from falsehood, and in sifting the evidence, but in real life that is not always the case.

In the event, his 12 month supervision order became a positive experience — got him off the streets, drew him into social activities like football training and body building — and he finally got through his final year at school against all early predictions. He's on a training course to be a bricklayer at present and we still keep in touch.

Christopher

After my reinstatement at school, there were traumatic events occurring in the life of Chris and his siblings. He had spent two week's respite from one aunt to another. Chris preferred living with this second aunt because of the freedom he was allowed, freedom that was not good for him. This aunt had permitted him to be out till late and had no idea where he was or what he might be getting up to. In fact, she didn't consider it very important to monitor him closely or know of his whereabouts through the evening, but felt that adults should 'always trust kids'. Although she wanted to offer a long-term home for Christopher and his brothers and sister, his social worker felt she had not the resources to see the task through, particularly when youngsters become challenging. In consequence, a foster home was found 15 miles away in an approved foster home of two parents with three late teenage daughters.

This was a very rushed affair. On taking Chris home on a Monday afternoon, he received a call on his mobile from his aunt asking if I would come into the house and contribute to a short meeting with the social worker to determine where Christopher could be placed in the light of him refusing to return to his former aunty. This had become a very distressing meeting in which his lenient aunt had not helped by offering unrealistic options that she knew Chris would want in the short term but which she also knew the social worker would oppose.

The social worker told his aunt and Christopher that the plan of the department had been to remove him and his one brother and sister to an alternative fostering placement not of the family. This news didn't go down well. Christopher became very upset as the aunt kept protesting against the plan, playing on his emotions.

On the Friday evening of that week, the social worker contacted his aunt to inform her that Chris would be moving to a non-family foster placement with his one brother and sister on the following Monday after school. I was asked to take him to this placement and he was very upset through not only being not first consulted, but also through having to leave friends and move from the area he had grown up in to be with new people in an unfamiliar location — far away from all family and friends (it was his friends that had been of chief concern).

At school on that day Chris nearly got excluded but I intervened to plead his case. In the next few days, I helped him move against much protestation of his aunt and initially of Christopher himself.

Eventually things turned out better than expected. After a few weeks into his new placement, there was a particularly troublesome incident that occurred on the same day as my first meeting with the fostering manager. Christopher had assaulted a boy in an English lesson after 'trying to stop a fight' in a classroom. What made it worse was that a senior teacher had recommended excluding him permanently from school.

The outcome was that Chris had to find another school. At a formal meeting Christopher's social worker and foster parents were asked to arrange a transfer to a more local school close by where he and his brother were living. All in all, Chris had lost both parents to heroin, and now he had lost his school and his personal friendships in the area where he had lived for most of his life. Chris took this announcement very badly and during the meeting stood to his feet, walked out and assaulted another boy unjustifiably to vent his anger — following this he was cautioned in court. Having lost everything, I determined he would not lose my support and loyalty. Although I now lost my after-school assistant, our future involvement together (looking initially improbable) continued.

A few months into his new placement, Chris had a new social worker, one I had known well from a previous placement. Knowing the details of the fabricated allegation against me, which was now resolved, there was no problem 'for him' over Chris still meeting with me through his foster carer. He was sufficiently confident for us to meet regularly. He had disdain for the principal officer of allegations against staff, as many of us had. I see him twice a week now where we have built a reconditioned engine for one of the old Rovers, and I take him motocross riding on his Suzuki RM85 — the dream of his childhood — around the country along with friends from his new school.

Postscript

I suppose the most contentious, and unresolved, issue was the recording on my CRB the graphic details of the accusation made against me. I had wanted to prove wrong what my association representative had said, at the close of the matter, which was that after an unfounded allegation life would never be the same again. However, in one sense he was wrong, but in another he was right. Yes, I was back in my original post with no incrimination or suspicion that I felt colleagues around me had, and yes I was back to my previous engagement with pupils outside of school, but in other respects things had altered. The school where I work underwent strategic changes in management, and an incoming head opposed any member of staff engaging with pupils socially outside school. In due course, the school safeguarding policy barred all social engagement with pupils in any context other than the professional one of teaching and learning. No doubt, this policy decision reflected not just my situation but was in keeping with the rising anxiety of being found culpable with respect to safeguarding and health and safety by managers.

Four years later, I applied for a counselling post in a sixth-form college and the education authority naturally required a CRB check. Although I was extremely well qualified for the post advertised, the fact that I was never shortlisted may be due to what was recorded on my CRB. I can't be certain about this but it is a possibility. At the current time, and in light of political change that is no less sensitive to child protection requirements for professionals in the workplace, there is no statutory timeframe to have removed from a CRB document any damning record of a false accusation made against an individual. In every section of the form, where it is asked for a disclosure of offences against children or vulnerable adults to be recorded, it is filled in with 'none known'. But in the section titled 'Any other relevant information', there is a detailed account, in stark prose, of what Alex had claimed had taken place between us, a paragraph of over 300 words. There is a sentence that closes with the rather lame expression by comparison, that says 'following an investigation the CPS found there was no case to answer, and the applicant returned to his post in September . . . '.

At one point, I asked Daniel to read the paragraph and answer as a prospective employer the question, quite objectively, whether he would employ a candidate after reading that record. Needless to say his answer was clearly no. There must be few other cases in British law where an individual remains permanently scarred if they are cleared and completely exonerated when accused of an offence than those applicable to child protection. Other issues of permanent branding relates to the PPOT minutes and my reinstatement as a foster carer.

The PPOT Minutes

In spite of three letters of request, I was never given a copy of any of the minutes of the three PPOT meetings, and had no early opportunity to challenge any of the deductions made without evidence by at least two of the professional attendees. In days of increased transparency and data protection legislation, I felt that this was unjustifiable and indefensible, and therefore wrote to the city solicitor following advice given me by the Fostering Network. After three written requests to chase up the case, I eventually received a doctored copy of the three PPOT minutes (Daniel having received his a few months earlier).[14]

All misgivings about attitudes and prejudices occurring in these meetings, which were previously made known to me by Daniel, were entirely justified after reading the minutes. A few comments were outrageously slanderous to say the least. I have no right of reply to the content of anything recorded in the minutes — apart from 'factual details' known to be false. Opinions are opinions, and I have no mandate to request alteration over those. They did reveal, however, some startling facts.

One was the manner of Alex's disclosure, which, having read in print, altered my earlier perception. Although it hasn't altered my story, had I have known then what I later discovered it would have considerably eased my tension at the time. I learned that it was not Alex but his girlfriend who had first gone to the police after their argument, and that he did not know she was going to the police but acted without his consent. Furthermore, she did not use the local station but a central one in the city centre, 7 miles from their home. I also learned that Alex was an unwilling and obstructive witness in interview. It occurred to me later on that not only was I never arrested at school, and not only had my computer never been seized for examination, my finger prints and DNA profile were never taken and put on file — the police, as my cousin's husband had said all along, were never going to take the accusation that seriously.

The minutes of the final meeting, together with a later conversation, revealed the grounds upon which the CPS had arrived at their decision not to charge me and to close the case. The CPS had recorded that:

- Both complainant and defendant were convincing in interview.
- The complainant had a history of dishonesty and violence
- The expert medical evidence pointed to some of the alleged actions by the defendant not being possible.
- The credibility of the complainant was an issue.
- In view of the above, the outcome therefore was that evidential criteria had not been met, and that in consequence no further action is to be taken.

Retirement From Fostering

The final chapter of my story centred upon my status as a foster carer. It is commonly recognised within fostering circles, that once an allegation has been made against a carer the local authority will never again place children in that particular home. There are no procedural guidelines for this, and it will nowhere be found in print, but it has been such a common experience amongst foster carers and the Fostering Network that it has become recognised as an unwritten working rule that following an allegation, founded or not, whether a defendant is charged or not, found guilty or acquitted, social workers will never place a child with that individual or couple again.

This has become a contentious issue, regularly raised in the media and in official fostering magazines, and it appears that my experience follows that of other unfortunate carers accused of child abuse by their foster children. As a result, independent fostering agencies recommend that a particular carer who has been subjected to a child abuse enquiry might as well retire from the service.

On four separate occasions, at approximately six-monthly intervals, delegated managers approached me inviting me to retire from the service. My answer initially was to suggest to each of the managers that they might cross me off the teenage fostering list. Their reply was they were not procedurally empowered to do this, but that retirement had to be the decision of the carer only. Yet to continue having me enrolled as a prospective foster carer with no prospect of a child being placed in my care would be for them a misuse of resources. Their reasons for me to retire were never stated as centering upon the allegation (though I knew differently), but on each occasion respective managers offered different, and sometimes contradictory, reasons for arriving at the decision, reasons that ranged from my age, to my disability and the unsuitability of the placement given the children who were currently on their books.

The final two meetings were getting us nowhere. A dance was occurring between two parties in power: my prerogative when to retire (which required a link-worker to review me monthly whether or not a child were placed in my home – the misuse of a resource); and their choice whether (never) to place a child in my care again.

I even at one point applied to an independent fostering agency and had two managers visit me very keen to take up my offer as a prospective carer. They were intrigued by my broad experience and wanted to sign me up straight away and place a teenager in my care, until I showed them my CRB and spoke of the unfounded allegation made against me three years previously. How the tone of eagerness altered was palpable. In spite of the fact that there had been an unprecedented advertising campaign due to the high demand for foster carers and the shortage of provision, they became instantly wary and defensive, attempting to close the meeting and make a rapid exit. Needless to say, my application was never taken up. [15]

I felt at this point, the game was up: my place within the city's Teenage Fostering Team was redundant, that there was no point in continuing. In our final meeting therefore, I offered them a way out.

"As I see the problem, we have reached an impasse. I know that your service will never place a child under my care again, and I'm aware that you would never admit that it's because of the allegation and what's recorded on my CRB, because to do so would contravene a sense of fairness and justice – I was never convicted and neither was I charged for abusing a minor. In consequence, you would like me to retire. You have a problem with this because you're not permitted to cross me off the books, and as a result I would be a tie on your resources by requiring a monthly review and an annual supervision whether or not a child were placed under my care. If your department were inspected, you would be criticised for having no paperwork to show for me being a member of the Teenage Fostering Service, and would thereby be accountable.

For my part, it is in my interest to retain membership, whether or not I intend to have a child placed in my care. The problem for me is that I have a damning report on my CRB, simply because of an allegation made against me, a report I have no authority to question or to defend, and if I were to apply for a job working with young people my CRB record would count against me and would considerably militate against a successful appointment. I cannot change what is written on my CRB, I can only request a slight modification to the wording if I believed it didn't reflect a true account (which I have actually done). I'm thereby penalised. However, while retaining my membership of the Teenage Fostering Team, there is a testament by an officially recognised body to my integrity as being a suitable person to be in the company of children and young people. That's why I have wished to remain on the books as an approved foster carer. So, where do we go from here?"

Both managers sat back with a look of frustration; the meeting had not gone according to plan, they both looked outwitted.

"Let me offer you a solution. I will retire if you write to me thanking me for all the years of service I have given to the young people of the city, a detailed and unblemished record of over 25 years service. Don't send me a general pro forma of gratitude, but instead a proper letter which requires you to go into my file and be very specific about my competence with respective children the department has placed in my care."

Within one week the letter arrived, and I carried out my pledge to retire from the fostering service. A further letter was sent from the teenage fostering panel acknowledging receipt of my letter and expressing further gratitude for my years of service. No adverse comment or instruction was ever given in regard to my continued engagement with Christopher.

NOTES

1. This book was written two years after the events on the advice of friends and colleagues that I had a story to tell. They felt that this would give encouragement to fellow professionals who had been similarly accused of child abuse to face their personal ordeal with courage and fortitude. *The Accused* is an account of my own experience of being under suspicion of historical child abuse and of having to face the exacting and prolonged procedures of a child abuse investigation.

   The book is written from a journal kept at the time, composed as a coherent record but with little editorial change. I not only wanted to capture the intensity of my emotions moment by moment, but to preserve the sense of felt injustice when knowing myself to be innocent but thinking that some (perhaps even close friends and colleagues) might presume me guilty on the basis of 'there's no smoke without fire'. There are grave implications for a foster carer/professional practitioner under suspicion of committing a criminal offence like that of child abuse, and only *the accused* fully appreciate the anxiety of being under suspicion.

2. There has been an unprecedented rise in accusations against teachers (http://teacherallegation.blogspot.com/), foster carers (between 3.5 & 31 per cent: www.fostering. net/sites/www.fostering.net/files/public/resources/reports/ advice_mediation_report_scotland.pdf) and particular

practitioners in the UK in recent years (Furedi and Bristow, 2008). Refined child protection legislation and an altered culture of high suspicion and litigation, amplified by a British media that sensationalises such cases, have resulted in a growing number of solicitors and legal firms promoting their services to 'injured victims' on a 'no-win no-fee' contractual basis.

So common has this been of late, that as many as one in four headteachers in the UK have had to manage serious allegations against their staff in secondary or high school. Even though as few as 98 per cent of allegations against teachers end in conviction, a significant number of pupils accuse teachers of being abusive. As many as one in five foster carers (particularly men) in the UK can expect to have an allegation made against them during their period of service.

The majority of allegations against professionals and guardians are not customarily of a sexual nature, but are more to do with poorly judged, or unfortunate, physical 'over-correction', losses of temper where physical constraint has been judged to be necessary (say in a fight between two pupils or inmates, or to prevent an angry youngster storming from the building and into an unsafe situation).

But in recent times a number of social workers have been accused, and convicted in some cases, of systematic and organised sexual abuse against children in residential settings, and even in the church there has been scandal where priests and religious clerics have abused their positions of trust by indulging in deviant sexual behaviour with children.

For years child abuse has been a hidden cancer within families and institutions, and for those who are guilty and who have covertly induced children into indecent sexual acts through subtle grooming, or who have physically beaten the innocents, public attention and tightening up of procedures has to be considered as laudable and long overdue, but what if *the accused* proves to be innocent? There is some evidence that the tide has come in too far. It might be thought that so long as investigatory systems are sufficiently rigorous and robust to catch even one abuser then it doesn't really matter if, say, ten others are wrongly accused or are acquitted after a trial, but there are other costs to be considered. Apart from the issue of social injustice, what if a less tangible effect is a withdrawal of volunteers and prospective foster carers coming forward for reasons of fear of false allegations? Indeed, recent reports in the UK have highlighted a withdrawal of teachers, foster carers and the voluntary sector from working with vulnerable people, and I don't think the rise in allegations against professionals is unrelated to these worrying trends

3. In later discussions, more facts about the details of Alex's report and motivation to speak with the police came to light, detail which has altered my perspective from that which I held at the time. Although I initially considered modifying the final narrative to incorporate the later, more accurate, detail, I later felt that I should remain true to what I had felt at the time, and this meant telling my story in light of slightly inaccurate, albeit believed, information.

4. Bisexuals often discover latent homosexual inclinations long after having struggled within heterosexual relationships and found them not fulfilling, and many in society are still of the view that individuals can 'become homosexual' rather than be born that way.

5. It has often been voiced by mothers of pupils at school that their sons are more affectionate than their daughters are, certainly around the ages of 11 and 12. I sensed that many boys at this point of development experience alienation as they witness male adult carers moving away from them and having no appropriate physical contact (certainly, this was my experience in childhood). They often experience an unhelpful withdrawal of tenderness at a point at which they are undergoing a confusion of love and human contact in an age of paradoxical sexual messages.

6. The problem is that whilst developmental psychologists highlight the importance of love and appropriate physical contact when nurturing a child (Biddulph, 1996; Biddulph and Stanish, 2008; Gerhardt, 2004), we happen to be living through a particular period in western society where a culture of extreme suspicion of malpractice exists and where particular taboos around sexuality and physical contact are dominant. Further, compensation and litigation claims are frequently made and have led to a series of procedural guidelines to help offset 'all risk' and any possibility of professionals being culpable of neglect or abuse, working rules which in themselves have become unworkable in some instances (safe-caring practice in

fostering) and incredibly expensive in others (supervised contact and homecare management).

Nowhere has this been more evident than in child protection procedures, where regulations on cautious and restrictive practice has left the most vulnerable and disadvantaged children with unmet emotional and social needs, not because of a lack of compassion and willingness but because the hands of altruistic adults have been tied so tightly together. As I discussed with my friend, I was acutely conscious of being in a particular arena which was wholly adversarial and amongst people who did not know my manner and way of life, people who might misjudge me as being a predator of vulnerable young people. In consequence, my reply to the officers, I reiterated to my friend, was to concede and agree that, 'in light of recent events, I would have to reconsider such affectionate responses as now being inappropriate'.

Conventions of 'safe-caring practice' were not as rigid 16 years ago as they are today, and although I acknowledge that abusers have previously taken advantage in that era of ignorance I would have to say that child protection protocols and investigating enquiries have penalised the many well-intentioned and genuine professional carers through failed attempts to catch the relatively few abusers of children and young people before tragedies had occurred.

7. A 'Persons in a Position of Trust' multi-agency strategy meeting is the statutory gathering in the UK of all principal officers, professionals and relevant bodies, to investigate

an accusation or raised concern of a professional person against a minor (www.nspcc.org.uk/inform/policyandpublicaffairs/policysummaries/abuseoftrust_wdf61907.pdf). Meetings are convened, organised and managed by the area office Child Protection Manager of social services, in liaison with the police, and in compliance with the Sexual Offences Act 2003.

8. Should Alex have been over 16 at the time, and now have been crying wolf at the age of 29, it could be ruled out on grounds that he was consenting to gay relations. But the Sexual Offences Act 2003 was brought in to check the loophole of professional people abusing their positions of power and escaping conviction after exploiting a trust a young person might have in them. It is not unknown, for example, for qualified teachers and youth workers, who may be taking up office at the age of 22, to have had sex with their 16-18 year old pupils or youth club members, since there may only be a difference of four to six years or so in their respective ages and levels of maturity. As a result, fifth-form and sixth-form pupils have flirted with and have had sexual relations with teachers in the past—some getting married and who are still together today. It was for this type of offence that the Act was composed, I believe.

9. What Jason was saying was that by going back to school, even if in my case it meant one year later, and even if it only meant for one term, it would be a positive statement when applying for further jobs, that by returning to the host

school it was an indication of justice having been seen to have occurred with no prejudice.

10. It is an article written in the local Mail on Wednesday 5 September 2007. It is written by Laura Clark, an education reporter, and is titled 'Teachers hit by tide of pupil lies'. The article reads:

> 'Teachers are facing a flood of false accusations from pupils, a survey revealed yesterday. Fifty-nine per cent of secondary heads said that they or at least one of their teachers had been falsely accused of bullying, neglect or verbal or physical abuse within the past three years. More than half said their school had been affected between two and five times . . . Head's leaders said false allegations could wreck personal lives and careers . . . There were also claims that a compensation culture exploited by 'no-win no-fee' lawyers is contributing to the rise in malicious allegations. The heads say parents are being encouraged to make claims in the hope of lottery-style payouts . . . A payout of a few thousand pounds can be a huge windfall to a family on a low income.'

11. On this last point, the public at large are led to suppose that paedophiles lurk on every street corner. Recent reports in Britain have drawn attention to the shortcomings of child protection policies and procedures in eliminating child abuse and the psychological barriers of healthy development of young people (Furedi and Bristow, 2008). If a person is penalised and made to feel 'guilty' for engaging

with young people, then whatever else was to come from my experience it was clear that heavy investigation with no sequel of praise and recognition of all that I had done over the past 30 years would lead more people to withdraw from voluntary service.

The media, quite naturally, feeds this frenzy and perpetuates the mythology of widespread paedophilia, but politicians have a responsibility to look at the kind of society that is developing. Why does parkland have restricted access? Why is it that no suitable play areas can be found in some deprived communities? Why is it that school playing fields have been sold for housing developments? And why are so many young people spending less time at play and more time in their bedroom in front of a computer screen? If over-anxious parents believe that this is the only safe way in which to bring up children then they are denying them the very opportunities of becoming socially well-rounded adults. These reports show that if trends continue then one in five young persons will grow up to have a serious mental disorder or a challenging behavioural problem.

12. The pamphlet is entitled *Protecting Children—Supporting Foster Carers: Dealing with an allegation*, and on page 10 a paragraph reads:

> Even if the local authority children's services decide not to undertake an enquiry, in accordance with their duties under section 47 of the Children Act 1989, the fostering service may decide to carry out their own investigation. Generally speaking, this is likely to take place only after the completion of any section 47 enquiries or police

investigations. In such circumstances, the fostering service should make clear, including in writing, the reasons for this further investigation . . . *Working Together to Safeguard Children* recognizes that the time this takes will depend on a variety of factors, but that fostering services should aim to have this review completed within 27 working days (10 days for the investigating officer to provide a report and two days for the fostering service to decide if a panel hearing is required). A panel should then be held within 15 days.

13. This is one of the difficulties with British law in that the jury's verdict is tantamount to the State assenting that the most accurate version of events is whatever supports the conviction, even though injured parties feel there may have been a gross injustice. The same applies to parole, whereby in order to get early release a convicted criminal has to confess that he or she has done what they have been convicted of, and that they are duly remorseful. If a person is innocent, though 'proved' guilty, and they preserve their dignity by never declaring otherwise, they suffer in two respects: a) no 'demonstration' of remorse in a pre-sentence report can result in a heavier sentence, and b) the likelihood of being turned down for parole.

14. Since the minutes contained essential information of a third party, namely Alex, and his circumstances, I am not allowed to view details relating to his situation. All such information appertaining to him is blotted out of the record, apart from that which is related material to the accusation

of child abuse. Similarly, I have no say on what is recorded on my current CRB document even though I remain an innocent, uncharged individual.

15. During this visit from the recruiting departments of the fostering agency, Christopher and his new friend (who by this time were 16 and 17 respectively) made a visit, and on entering the house and being courteous they waited in the kitchen till our meeting finished. At one point, the milkman arrived for payment, and Christopher's friend politely knocked the door and entered. I called him in and gave my wallet to pay the bill. He did not disturb our meeting, but gave me my wallet back after they had left.

After reading through my CRB document, the tone of the meeting altered and it was palpable. One of the officers asked me a direct question: "Richard, you've offered a placement to support young people in the final stages of fostering, in assisting them to acquire self-supporting skills. What would you do if we placed a young lady of 16 with you and . . ."

"Now wait a minute, I don't think it's appropriate to place a young girl in my care, me being a single male foster carer . . ."

"Oh yes of course, suppose we place a young man of 16 with you and during the early evening he was a little fed up and said to you, 'Get stuffed. I'm not cooking my tea tonight, you do it; that's what you get paid for!' What would happen?"

I sat back in the chair for a moment's reflection and said, "Well, I suppose he'd go hungry!"

"But don't you think we have a responsibility to meet their nurturing needs?"

"Yes, and we have a responsibility to prepare them for independence. I'm not denying them food, there will be plenty in the fridge and freezer."

I realised at that point I had given them the wrong answer. "You see," I continued, "this is the problem. Young people in care, though damaged, can be manipulative, especially those having been in the system for some time, and those in children's homes. At the age of 18, a foster child will be left principally to stand on their own two feet, and where will your agency be in the long-term? You would have closed the file and be working with other, younger, foster children . . . I keep contact with all the fostered children that have been under my care throughout their late teens and into adulthood."

It was interesting to read the written report of our meeting. This particular conversation and its sequel were never put in writing, but instead there was another objection recorded as the reason for my rejection as a prospective foster carer. The report said that I had failed to exercise 'safe-caring practice', and the example that was cited was that of Christopher's friend at 18 not returning my wallet and yet having the initiative to pay the milkman the bill with the minimum of disturbance to our meeting.

At a final meeting convened by the department to encourage me to resign, I drew attention to this and said to the two workers the following: "There was clearly a different mindset between myself over what I regard as essential when fostering teenagers compared with the two workers. For me, it's about trust. The two workers were unable to assess through observation the trust that Christopher and his friend had evidently placed in me, and I in them. They could only view such behaviour sceptically, as though I would, indeed, allow any teenager to take my wallet without knowing something of their personality, without having tested them over a period of time—I am no gullible fool."

I went on to explain to them how I had successfully managed an independent children's home during my 30s when there was a severe breakdown between the children and staff (in fact the senior house parents walked out after a big argument). The first thing I did was to remove all the locks from the rooms, including the office and each bedroom (even the fridge and freezer were padlocked). We had regular council meetings to discuss issues, and it was clear that what they had needed, indeed what they have been deprived of for most of their lives, was trust.

"You see, we cannot live without trust. And no matter how untrustworthy some youngsters may be, we have to instil trust in them and see that as a basis of our relationships. Those two workers could not see that; whether they were looking for some ulterior reason to decline my fostering application, I have no idea, but what I was criticised for was over the trust I had instilled within them. Young people rise to trust, and that has been the basis of every successful fostering placement I have had.

Issues Arising

One friend suggested that I should represent each side of the contentious issue of child abuse allegations for balance; to reflect the social worker's position in having to investigate the case as well as that of the defendant faced with being suspected or charged. After considering the suggestion, I felt this would be difficult.

The pressures and responsibilities for investigating social service managers are considerable in our media-driven age, obsessed as it is with publicising professional incompetence, but I think their side would be represented more effectively if a person occupying such a position were to write about that perspective other than me. I would in spite of this acknowledge that social workers have to work under unenviable conditions where error of judgement is unremittingly exposed and where success is rarely acknowledged. Social workers locally are under-resourced and have unmanageable caseloads.

Investigating officers are faced with immensely difficult decisions of whether to remove some children from their parents for their 'protection', where emotional attachments are strong and where screaming and shouting often makes this a harrowing ordeal for them personally. And if they let matters lie, they risk unrelenting press and television coverage, where journalists and politicians take the moral high ground and weigh up their every decision from a 'holier than thou' position. It is little wonder then that being a social worker is a difficult job in modern times.

Anyone taking the time to read this book who may be under suspicion or have been charged or may be awaiting a decision of a jury that will discharge or convict him or her will feel, as I have done over the period, that their whole life is suspended and that their integrity is held in question by an imaginary if not a real audience. Undoubtedly, every teacher or foster carer, or other professional who may have had an allegation made against them, will find it extremely distressing, as indeed I have done. If they are guilty, then the cost of their anxiety is minimal in comparison to that of an innocent minor who through present and future development will have to bear the pain and psychological scars that could remain with them and affect their relationships for the rest of their lives.

Anybody having been accused of child abuse knows whether or not they are guilty. *The Accused* is a personal account of my claim to be innocent, but it is also a story of the dilemma of how necessary procedures affect an individual at the deepest level of psychological and social wellbeing. The reader will have questioned whether or not I had been guilty of what had been claimed by Alex; that is human nature, I suppose, and I have to live with that. I have no control over my reader's opinion. In closing this account, I think there are a number of issues that surround my story, and below I give a brief summary of what stands out for further discussion.

Conflicting 'Truths' and 'Different Mindsets'

'What is truth?', asked a Roman governor of a Galilean. The pursuit of truth is an elusive endeavour. In cases of child abuse, as in rape, where two testimonies conflict, someone has to decide on whose account is the most plausible. In the absence of corroborative evidence, or reliable independent witnesses, the task becomes quite a challenge.

Managing cases in law is quite different from arriving at decisions of justice in school and in case conferences. The CPS, the police and the judicial system, operate from the principle of what can be proved 'beyond all reasonable doubt', whereas pastoral teachers and social workers occasionally operate from the principal of 'the balance of probabilities'. However, for those practitioners holding a particular office, I think it is possible to discern that their basis of decision-making is not wholly a neutral exercise, largely because their occupied position (shaped by workaday experience) in conducting their work has tended to predispose them towards taking a particular stance, which through reinforcement develops into a particular mindset that is commonly recognised by those practitioners outside the social work profession. This is not a criticism, but an observation. The stances of teachers and policemen over social judgements are also recognisable in that although they are individuals they collectively have predispositions that are largely shaped through the nature of their work.

I recognise I'm treading on dangerous ground in making such stereotypical comments, nevertheless, on nearly every child protection course I've attended—generally conducted by social work presenters—it has been regularly voiced that 99.9% of allegations of child abuse made by minors have turned out to be correct. If indeed this were the case, then the particular mindset of the practitioner would be understandable, but in my experience and in that of other senior teachers who have had to manage allegations against their staff such figures are exaggerated.

In addition to this observation, I have failed to find any validated research to support the claim.

Teachers have a different mindset when working with children and young people. They recognise that there are other forces that can come into play when a child makes an allegation, that indeed children and young people can be highly manipulative. High levels of specific offences carried out by particular ethnic groups can also influence the mindset of a policeman. In a sense, I am saying that developing a particular predisposition and mindset is unavoidable.

Does this not argue the case for more extensive self-awareness training on how practitioners arrive at conclusions from unconscious predispositions, and on how practice judgments are arrived at from a philosophical basis?

Values of Class when Determining 'What is Abusive'

Throughout the three-month period, I was conscious of being judged by standards of 'safe-caring practice' in the present rather than by conventions of 16 years ago, and by differences more to do with class than anything else—hugging teenagers, permitting them to visit my home, not insisting that Patrick's mother should inspect the sleeping arrangement before allowing her son to stay etc.

There are class values underpinning views on appropriate child-rearing methods and failures: some parents, it is argued, bring up their children 'properly', meeting all their social, physical and emotional needs, and others are 'neglectful' or 'abusive'. Apart from an obvious case of a child's death, are there not class and cultural issues centering on referral take-up in cases of 'neglect', 'physical over-correction' and even 'decency' — attitudes of paraded nakedness within families, mixed gender bedroom sharing (even bed-sharing — known as top-and-tailing) within working-class family groupings of teenagers, and sexual experimentation amongst sibling children?

Showing male affection is another issue in our time where cultural as well as class barriers determine what is and what is not appropriate. Is hugging teenagers by non-family adults in cases where both parties share a mutual bond necessarily such a harmful practice and a crossing of professional boundaries?

Males as 'Abusers'

In a zealous interest to protect all children in every conceivable situation, which I do not question, we seem to be moving towards a state of paranoia in trying to create an unrealistic, risk-free social environment by setting up the most impractical of rules to offset not only the possibility of suspicion but also of any chance of accusations being made against professionals.

I am aware that males in the main tend to be abusers but this is not exclusively the case. An example comes to mind of a tennis coach in the West Midlands who had been convicted and sentenced for nearly three years of sexually molesting a young girl. The court heard how the coach had engaged this pupil in oral sex, had slept with her at Bournemouth and had drawn her into 'lesbian activities' over a period of time, that she had worn the child's knickers, and, most alarmingly, that she was allowed to continue a professional involvement with her in spite of them being observed by officials at the tennis club in a toilet cubicle. The court heard that the young girl's mother had also discovered them together, catching her daughter naked in bed with the tennis coach engaged in oral sex and molestation whilst she was only 13 years of age (her mother had returned home early one evening from a party).

Surprisingly, her mother still sanctioned the defendant to coach her daughter. It was interesting to read the press reaction to this case, as many commentators had noted. This serious assault was not reported as an act of paedophilia, or as rape by some journalists, but as 'lesbian sex' with a 'minor' by a 'responsible adult in a position of power'. The coach had exploited the infatuation of a youngster with herself. Should this have been a man, not only would he have received a sterner sentence but would have been branded as a paedophile and Schedule 1 Sex Offender. Other, more recent, cases include female teachers and nursery staff abusing children in their care (http://www.mirror.co.uk/news/uk-news/tennis-coach-jailed-for-lesbian-sex-518095: http://news.bbc.co.uk/1/hi/england/8345756.stm).

Safe-caring Practice

During one discussion with Christopher's foster carers, I became aware of the current expectations of 'safe-caring practice' for foster carers (I say 'expectations' because although the guidance is not mandatory, or written up as regulatory practice, there is broad discouragement of physical touch perpetuated through training or link worker consultation). Hugging and kissing children and young people in care has become a thorny issue where there's a lack of clarity in what is regarded as appropriate 'safe-touch'.

Safe-touch

Legislation following Victoria Climbié's horrific death not only stipulates who is allowed to care for a child, but how care should be administered, including holding, hugging and physical touch. In 2004-5, Heather Piper and colleagues at Manchester Metropolitan University conducted an ESRC-funded study into the 'very problematics of touching between children and professionals' (Furedi and Bristow, 2008).

Piper's team investigated the way in which UK childcare professionals experienced the tension between children's need for nurturing contact and the fear that such contact may be interpreted as 'abusive'. Reported injunctions included, 'always having a second adult witness intimate care routines, minimising cuddling young children, even requiring particular ways of doing this, such as the sideways cuddle (to avoid frontal bodily contact)'.

This study reflected the uncertainty over how appropriate standards should be met during Ofsted inspection processes combined with a section of the National Care Standards that encourages staff to 'avoid putting themselves in a situation that might lead to allegations made against them'. In other words, these bodies did not advocate 'no touch' as such but had created policies that would lead to a process of second-guessing what is appropriate and what might be judged by an overseeing manager as being 'risky' and open to an allegation of abuse.

Jean Bond (CCYP, June 2007) reported on novel residential work in Derbyshire with criminal at-risk young people, and one telling feature came to light in a debrief forum for parents. The young people voiced to more than 30 people their prepared accounts of what they had gained most from the course, and top of their list was 'having cuddles from people'. Jean glanced at the faces of bemused parents from their declarations, an experience which caused her to ponder on the connection between 'emotional availability' and 'criminality'.

Apart from hazy and non-committal guidance on the 'hugging, embracing and kissing' of children in foster care outlined in my story above, two further areas where concern had been shared with me by current foster carers were over transporting foster children to their respective schools or social functions, and the requirements of adults and non-fostered youngsters being in the same bedroom occupied by fostered children. Some of this guidance is wholly impracticable.

Gender management of 'Looked after Children'

The first feature of safe-caring practice that has become unworkable is that a male carer is not strictly allowed to be alone with a female 'looked after child' in a car. In practice, in Christopher's case, this had meant that his foster father had to arrange to deliver his older sister, Amanda, at her school before him at his in such a manner that was considerably inconvenient to satisfy the requirement; that in this case, Christopher should always be dropped off last and be in the car at all times whilst his sister was there.

Why should this not apply to the opposite gender? When Chris and his sister were picked up after school, where it was more practical for the foster mother to pick them both up, the same conditions did not apply. It was not judged as being necessary for a female carer not to be alone with Christopher in the car as was the case with her husband with Amanda. Now these requirements are making very loud statements about gender discrimination, and it has surprised me that this guidance has remained intact and not been challenged.

Imagine all the logistical difficulties in a foster placement through having to maintain in every respect the condition that the male carer should never be alone with his female foster child.

Should, for example, a foster father be compelled to remove himself from the sitting room if he is alone with a female foster child? Should he make an exit to prevent all possibility of an allegation being made against him?

What would happen if the female carer was ill, or otherwise engaged, should the male carer ask a neighbour next door to accompany him to a doctor, to the dentist or even to hospital in the event of an accident or an illness or for treatment? How indeed can a family — trying to replicate 'normal' family relations — function this way?

Are we going to find another stipulation of safe-caring practice come into force whereby no female can any longer transport a young girl alone in the car to school or anywhere else without a third-party being present?

Should we expect new guidance requiring female carers never to enter a bedroom of a young boy or girl in foster care if they are ill in order to satisfy the requirement?

Some fostering agencies apply 'stricter expectations' than is set down in council run fostering teams (not letting teenagers out, or sanctioning 15 year olds going to school on a cycle etc.), and I am not surprised that so many foster carers have confessed to me privately that they unashamedly have not always followed the 'guidance' given, and for very good reason.

Headteachers in some schools have already begun to caution staff against being with pupils alone with them in a car, either to transport them home if they are ill, or to exclude them to avoid a serious fight after school. Taxi drivers are not permitted to transport young girls from foster or children's homes without an accompanying female adult.

One thing that is fairly certain, in cases where advice has not been followed by the letter, is that foster carers can rely upon one certain fact: that the management will withdraw support from them if an allegation has been made.

Stigmatising 'Looked after Children'

One requirement of safe-caring practice is that no child in foster care is permitted to 'sleepover' at a friend's house or to have a friend sleepover in the bedroom without police checks on the family. Children in foster care are expected to have their own private bedroom space and to have no other person apart from a biological sibling in that bedroom at whatever age and in whatever circumstances at the same time. This means in practice that for children in care—who are already stigmatized—they have the further insult to feel their difference by a system that denies them privileges that most of their peers have by custom. This would mean that Christopher (as a looked after child) would not be able to have a friend stay over with him at his foster home at night, and neither would he be able to even have his cousin (a non-looked after child) sleep in or share the same bedroom overnight.

It would also mean that should the foster carer have one of their own children of the same age, or even younger, they could not only never sleep in the same bedroom for companionship, but should never even enter the bedroom whilst the foster child was there alone, not even to chat or to watch a TV program. Are not these requirements unreasonable and over-reactive?

Shortcomings of Child Protection Procedures

Social workers have a hard-press when children under their charge die at the hands of their carers, and such cases have led to reform. The legislation brought into force from inadequate service communication following the Victoria Climbié case and that of 'Child Peter' has been considerable, albeit after the horse had bolted. Yet child protection enquiries still remain inconsistent in different parts of the country. There is variation from area office to area office, from worker to worker and from referral to referral.

It is generally recognised that the legislative changes following the Climbié case would not necessarily have prevented a similar thing happening again ('Child Peter'), and further that the structures arising from that catastrophe have had the effect of making fostering largely unworkable with older children. From the Climbié case, Lord Laming's Inquiry led to Children's Safeguarding Boards and increased bureaucracy, now with 'Child Peter's' death at the hands of his mother there has resulted a call for more 'intuitive judgement' and 'less bureaucracy', the very cause, it was argued, that had led to the murder of Victoria Climbié. Round in circles we go.

Most allegations against teachers are not of a sexual nature, but are more to do with physical 'over-correction' of pupils refusing discipline. I have supported teachers where tempers had been lost and what I would call 'unintended physical contact' had resulted, when, for example, restraining a pupil to stop a fight, or preventing them from leaving a room against an instruction, where the intention is not to hurt or harm but to keep order and maintain control. The question is where the balance is to be drawn between protecting children and applying common sense when tempers are lost.

Judging what is effective childcare management in the UK for 'looked after children' has become confused and unclear, where many professionals feel divided between what they feel is necessary for the well-being of the child, and exercising sufficient cautionary distance in order to avoid an allegation. All carers and professionals informed on the nature of infant-teenager brain development and nurturing needs of children have a sense of what is required, but the legislative requirements stand as an obstacle to their intuitive judgement. The state is reluctant to grant freedom to a carer to exercise exclusively their own judgement, and this results in regular tension, tension which leads ultimately to an unfortunate but predictable situation where volunteers withdraw from service, teachers seldom engage with pupils beyond their contracted obligations and foster carers have to fight a daily battle of meeting their child's needs and satisfying the requirements of the management.

At one time, care staff in children's homes gave up their free time to engage inmates in their own hobbies and interests during off-duty hours. This no longer occurs. At one time, teachers could socialise freely with their pupils and parents out of the classroom. Current safeguarding policies now ban such activity. At one time, foster parents exercised their own intuitive judgement on routine matters like where their children might sleep-over, or what high-risk sports they may engage in, just as they would with their own children. This is no longer permitted without consultation with key workers and the requirement of CRB checks. Whilst every attempt to safeguard children and young people must be made, particularly in institutional settings in the wake of what has come to light in recent times, a pertinent question has to be whether the legislation is securing those safeguards or providing a false sense of security, and, further, whether the legislation is having unintended consequences.

Legislation and the elimination of risk

Increased legislation does not avoid all possibility of risk. In needing to learn lessons from the Soham murders and the Climbié enquiry, the official response was the 'Every Child Matters' policy framework. ContactPoint was created which was a form of vetting on a centralised database at a cost of £224m. Schools, health authorities, social services, the police and other relevant authorities were to store information about every child in the country. Information could be accessed and shared between these agencies. However, this has not prevented one child every week dying in the UK as a result of parental abuse, it wouldn't have stayed Ian Huntley's hand and it didn't save 'Child Peter' coming to an untimely death.

Two reports were published in 2008. One was by a research team that concluded that children are no longer experiencing necessary opportunities for playing during their early development. It recognised that children learn social roles, develop their own sense of independence, learn to communicate with each other, learn to share and to give and to acquire the necessary physical exercise and social engagement through play. The other report highlighted:

- Shortcomings of the Criminal Records Bureau
- The stressful inconvenience for prospective volunteers having to undergo a CRB check
- A widespread distrust of government technical competence
- The recognition that vetting has put off some prospective volunteers and delayed the process of involvement for most volunteers
- The recognition that ultimately CRB checks cannot prevent people from committing an offence after the check has been made.

(Furedi and Bristow, 2008)

The vetting procedures have led to a tendency for adults to mistrust their own intuitive judgement, a judgement that proved pretty accurate in the past; it has led also to a deskilling of adult management of children and young people. Adults no longer feel responsible for the welfare of young people who are not their own children, and there has grown a climate of responsibility aversion, which has led to disastrous results.

High-profile news stories in 2007 illustrate the paralysing effect of over-reactive child protection measures. Paul Waugh, a coastguard in Cleveland, climbed down a cliff against high winds to rescue a stranded 13-year-old girl without waiting to fit a safety harness. He was criticised by the Maritime and Coastguard Agency for failing to meet health and safety procedures, and has resigned in disgust as a result. Jordan Lyon, a 10-year-old boy, died after jumping into a pond to rescue his stepsister from drowning. Two police community support officers failed to help because they lacked 'training in water rescue', a decision supported as proper by Greater Manchester Police. A 2-year-old girl disappeared from a nursery and was drowned in a garden pond. A bricklayer had driven past as she wandered through the village. "She wasn't walking in a straight line. She was tottering. I kept thinking, 'Should I go back?'" He told the inquest into the child's death, "One reason I did not go back is because I thought someone would see me and think I was trying to abduct her" (Furedi and Bristow, 2008).

This process of 'playing safe' is the natural result for adults to avoid suspicion of child abuse and to meet stringent health and safety regulations in order to protect themselves from negative labelling of paedophilia. Another unintended consequence of increased child protection bureaucracy following the case of 'Child Peter' was a knee-jerk reaction resulting in a significant rise of children being taken into care in the three weeks following the child's death, in spite of the individual costs (now escalating to £4000/week each case) and the unavailability of foster carers.

What being under suspicion following an accusation of child abuse does in effect is to seriously discourage people like me from having any involvement with children and young people other than a professionally distant one to earn a living.

An attitude of 'you must be mad to get involved with kids if this is what can happen' develops.

There has to be a middle way in managing child protection, between aligning oneself with a defendant in collusion and over-reactionary legislation and injustice. Authors of a recent report (Furedi and Bristow, 2008) have recommended the need to have enlightened policy which puts greater trust in the ability of professionals and volunteers to act on their instincts and less pressure upon them to cover their backs and less policy: putting a halt to the juggernaut of regulation and behaviour codes that make voluntary organisations increasingly difficult to run, and volunteers resentful and unsure of themselves. There is also a need for sustained public discussion of issues raised.

Note

'Child Peter' was a seventeen-month child who was discovered dead from a fracture/dislocation of the thoraco-lumbar spine whilst in the care of his mother. In the home at the time, along with his mother, were her boyfriend, their lodger, his three children and his 'girlfriend' of 15 years. Child Peter died in spite of a multi-agency Child Protection Plan being in place by Haringey Social Services (the same council which managed the Climbié case), and in spite of frequent visits to the family by the police and social workers, and in spite of three medical inspections including a paediatrician called in to carry out a detailed examination of the child's injuries, emotional state and development. No concerns were ever raised by health or school over the mother's other three children living in the home. Practitioners' testified to the hyperactive and boisterous play of the young boy, and I suspect that if a tragedy hadn't have occurred there might never have been a case to answer.

REFERENCES

Biddulph, S. (1996) *The Secret of Happy Children*. London: Thorsons.

Biddulph, S. and Stanish (2008) *Raising Boys: Why Boys Are Different — And How to Help Them Become Happy and Well-Balanced Men*. London: Celestial Arts.

DfES (2006) *Protecting Children — Supporting Foster Carers: Dealing with an allegation*. Nottinghamshire: DfES Publications.

Furedi, F. and Bristow, J. (2008) *Licensed to Hug: How Child Protection Policies Are Poisoning the Relationship Between the Generations and Damaging the Voluntary Sector*. London: Civitas.

Gerhardt, S. (2004) *Why Love Matters: How Affection Shapes a Baby's Brain*. London: Routledge.

Greenfield S. (2004) *Tomorrow's People: How 21st Century Technology is Changing the Way we Think and Feel*. London: Penguin.

Jean Bond (2007) 'Criminal risk: rebalancing the odds', June 2007. BACP, Rugby: *Counselling Children and Young People*: pp. 42-4.

Jodi Picoult (2001) *Salem Falls*. Ney York: Washington Square Press.

Masters, A. (2006) *Stuart: A life backwards*. London: Harper Perennial.

Shriver, L. (2003) *We Need to Talk About Kevin*. London: Serpent's Tail.

Sobel, D. (2000) *Galileo's Daughter: A Historical Memoir of Science, Faith, and Love.* London: Fourth Estate.

Thorne, B. (2005) *Loves Embrace: An Autobiography of a Person-Centred Therapist.* Ross-on-Wye, Herefordshire: PCCS Books.

Tillich, P. (1952) *The Courage to Be* (second edition: 2000). London: Yale Nota Bene, Yale University Press.